Students Helping Students

Steven C. Ender
Fred B. Newton

Students Helping Students

A Guide for Peer Educators on College Campuses

JOSSEY-BASS
A Wiley Company
www.josseybass.com

Published by

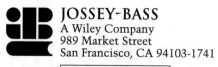
JOSSEY-BASS
A Wiley Company
989 Market Street
San Francisco, CA 94103-1741

www.josseybass.com

Jossey-Bass books and products are available through most bookstores. To contact Jossey-Bass directly, call (888) 378-2537, fax to (800) 605-2665, or visit our website at www.josseybass.com.

Substantial discounts on bulk quantities of Jossey-Bass books are available to corporations, professional associations, and other organizations. For details and discount information, contact the special sales department at Jossey-Bass.

We at Jossey-Bass strive to use the most environmentally sensitive paper stocks available to us. Our publications are printed on acid-free recycled stock whenever possible, and our paper always meets or exceeds minimum GPO and EPA requirements.

Library of Congress Cataloging-in-Publication Data

Ender, Steven C.
    Students helping students: a guide for peer educators on college campuses/Steven C. Ender, Fred B. Newton.—1st ed.
       p. cm.—(The Jossey-Bass higher and adult education series)
    Adaptation of: Students helping students/Steven C. Ender, Sue Saunders-McCaffrey, Theodore K. Miller. © 1979.
    Includes bibliographical references (p.) and index.
    ISBN 0-7879-4459-9 (alk. paper)
    1. Peer counseling of students. 2. Peer-group tutoring of students. I. Newton, Fred B. II. Title. III. Series.
    LB1027.5 .E52 2000
    371.4'047—dc21

                                       99-059007

PB Printing 10 9 8 7 6 5 4 3 2   FIRST EDITION

Contents

Preface

This text provides a resource for students who are in training to become peer educators. Many thousands of students are now serving their peer group in an array of helping positions on college and university campuses, and their success is largely dependent upon the skills they develop in training.

Students now serve as peer health educators, peer counselors, peer advisers, resident assistants, peer tutors, supplemental instruction leaders, orientation leaders, and group facilitators, and they fill many other positions on college and university campuses. They are making a positive and lasting difference for students with whom they have contact. The role is one of great significance and you are to be congratulated for choosing to become a peer educator, for you too will make a difference in the lives of others on your campus.

To be effective as a peer educator, you will find it necessary to examine your personal strengths and weaknesses as a helping person, know problem-solving strategies, and learn and practice specific helping skills. In this text we present a comprehensive range of helping skills that apply to all peer educators regardless of their campus role. Additionally, the text describes problem-solving strategies that will be useful when you work with individuals and groups. It also guides you in the process of examining and developing the personal qualities you will need for success in your new role. We have not been able to cover everything anyone might need to know in all the varieties of tasks peer educators perform, but we believe that the topics addressed in this text provide a baseline of skill development that is essential for any campus role.

Structure of the Book

Each chapter in this text contains elements of theory, skill building, and application. You will discover a list of learning objectives at the beginning of each chapter, followed by text, and then by summary questions. Many of the learning objectives can be achieved through a reading of the text material only. To master other learning objectives you will need to participate in training activities or complete exercises outside the training experience, and these will be assigned by your trainer. Also, within each chapter you will discover personal reflection segments and instructions for exercises. The personal reflection points should be completed as you read the text. Your trainer will assign textbook exercises for you to focus on. It is our belief that learning helping skills is most effective when the peer educator understands the content knowledge from a conceptual framework, receives specific instruction on how to practice helping skills, and has the opportunity, through experiences in an active training setting, to apply those skills. Because of this belief we have designed this training program to include both active and reflective learning techniques.

Helping skills are complex. Many of the areas covered in the text could easily form the basis of a course or text in themselves. In most instances, it is impossible to cover in depth each helping skill topic in a single training program. Therefore, our goal is to provide you with a level of exposure sufficient for you to assess and take advantage of the resources that you bring from your past experience and those you will gain through this training and through your efforts as a peer educator. We review the essential helping skills and practices applicable to most peer educator settings in an effort to stimulate greater personal awareness on your part of the benefits of extending your learning possibilities. We also suggest specific application of the skills introduced, and provide advice and exercises designed to assist you as you understand yourself and your possibilities, capabilities, and limitations in the helping situation.

This text consists of ten chapters. The first four are intended to provide the core helping foundation and personal knowledge that we believe are necessary for later skill development. As we have said, competent helping people first know themselves and the personal strengths and weaknesses they bring to the helping relationship. With this concept in mind, the first four chapters will require you to be somewhat introspective in regard to yourself, the world around you, and your communication skills as a helping person.

In Chapter One, "Peer Educators on the College Campus," we provide an overview of the role you are taking up. We review the extent to which peer interventions are used on college campuses and how peer programs have been effective. For the purpose of training we introduce the *What, So what, Now what* personal process model for integrating new skills and information. We also explore the importance of being a role model and mentor for those with whom you interact on your campus.

As a peer educator you will be assisting other students who are facing personal challenges of all types. In Chapter Two, "Student Maturation and the Impact of Peers," we explore the types of personal changes and challenges most college-age students experience. The concept of challenge-and-response dynamics as it relates to and stimulates personal change is explored. This chapter points out the powerful variables found on college campuses that create challenges for students, thereby having the potential to positively affect their personal development. In this chapter, you are also encouraged to reflect on your own development and maturation level, assessing your strengths and considering strategies to improve areas that you note for improvement.

In Chapter Three, "Intercultural Competence," Ata Karim focuses on the importance of realizing that on college campuses with diverse student populations, it is essential to be accepting and understanding of individual differences and to learn skills in cross-cultural communication. You will be asked to explore your acceptance of differences and issues of diversity. This is a critical area to explore given the range of individual differences found on most college campuses.

Chapter Four, "Interpersonal Communication Skills: Creating the Helping Interaction," explores the significance of effective listening and responding skills, emphasizing both verbal and nonverbal communication patterns. Core helping areas of empathy, respect, and warmth are defined. Basic responses in helping interactions are explained with specific examples. This chapter stresses the importance of personal feelings and the power of exploring affective dimensions when working with individuals who seek your help. Most important, you will learn that helping others with personal concerns is accomplished by being a competent, empathic, nonjudgmental listener.

Chapter Five, "Problem Solving with Individuals," covers the topic of assisting others through the use of active problem-solving approaches. The integration of communication skills with a problem-solving model is also presented, as are other specific problem-solving techniques.

Chapter Six, "Understanding Group Process," presents an overview of group development and group dynamics. You are challenged in this chapter to heighten your awareness and subsequent attention to group communication patterns, normative behavior, decision processes, cohesion, and individual coordination toward group task. Attention to group process is a major ingredient in making improvements in the functioning level of a group.

Chapter Seven, "Leading Groups Effectively," looks at the necessary characteristics of being an effective leader as well as covering the very practical nuts and bolts of conducting productive group meetings and making group presentations. Skills and methods for organizing, facilitating, and solving problems with groups are explored.

In Chapter Eight, "Strategies for Academic Success," Sally Lipsky addresses the issues and methods that students use to succeed in their classes. We believe college peer educators, regardless of their campus role, should model and be able to transmit strategies for academic success and intellectual development. This chapter explores very practical strategies for time management, study, reading, note taking, and test preparation. It introduces academic success strategies and discusses the need for modeling so as to transfer these methods to other students. The concept of a "Learner Packet" is also modeled in the chapter. The Learner Packet is an excellent tool for student helpers to utilize as they work with individual students through the use of prepared handouts.

In Chapter Nine, "Using Campus Resources and Referral Techniques," you will learn to recognize student problems that may require the assistance of other helping agencies on your campus or in the surrounding community. You will also be introduced to techniques for assessing the resources available to students in your area, as well as to techniques for making a referral so that the students who ask your help will understand that you are helping and not brushing them off.

Chapter Ten, "Ethics and Strategies for Good Practice," presents our ideas regarding ethical behavior and specific behavioral guidelines for peer educators—topics we believe you need to consider to guide your helping interventions with others.

The Epilogue of this text summarizes some next steps or post-training activities. No one training experience can do it all, and we believe that anyone working as a helping person can benefit from in-service training activities and continuous improvement.

Acknowledgments and Conclusion

We take great pleasure in offering this resource to you. This text is an adaptation of an early manual for training peer helpers, *Students Helping Students: A Training Manual for Peer Helpers on the College Campus*. That earlier text was cowritten by one of the current authors, Steven C. Ender, and was published by Student Development

Associates of Athens, Georgia, in 1979. Other writers of the earlier text were Theodore K. Miller and Sue Saunders-McCaffrey. We are grateful to these authors for releasing the copyright of *Students Helping Students* to us so that we could develop this updated and expanded text.

As you begin the process of learning effective helping skills we encourage you to explore yourself and your potential. It is this same exploration and encouragement that you will give others on a daily basis in your peer educator role. We hope you find both training and serving others to be as exciting and personally relevant as we have in our own lives. The twenty-first century will challenge students like no other in the past. The complexity of life and its associated demands can take a toll. You are in a position to make a difference in the life experiences of others. We challenge you to make the most of this exciting life experience!

January 2000

Steven C. Ender
Indiana, Pennsylvania
Fred B. Newton
Manhattan, Kansas

The Authors

STEVEN C. ENDER is a professor in the Learning Center at Indiana University of Pennsylvania. He earned his M.Ed. in student personnel services in 1976 and Ed.D. in counseling and human development services in 1981 from the University of Georgia.

He has served on the faculty at the University of Georgia and Kansas State University. He has also served in administrative positions at IUP along with his faculty appointment. He has designed and implemented learning enhancement programs at three universities and has taught on both the undergraduate and graduate level. He has cowritten and edited six books in the areas of academic advisement, student affairs contributions to student learning, and training undergraduates to serve as student paraprofessional peer educators. He has also authored or coauthored fourteen book chapters and sixteen articles in professional journals.

Ender is presently an elected member of editorial boards representing two national journals—the *Journal of College Student Development* and the National Academic Advising Association's journal, *NACADA*. For six years he served as an associate editor for the *Journal of College Student Development*. Since 1989, along with his other university responsibilities, Ender has developed, implemented and managed secondary–higher education partnership programs with eight school districts representing forty high schools. This partnership program is designed to promote high school graduation and college success for inner-city schoolchildren who are academically at risk.

FRED B. NEWTON is director of counseling services and professor of counseling and educational psychology at Kansas State University. He received his doctorate in counseling psychology from the University of Missouri–Columbia in 1972. At the University of Missouri he was on an EPDA (Education Professions Development Act) fellowship. He also has a master's degree in student personnel services from Ohio State University in 1968.

Newton's early career included teaching and coaching in the public schools, serving as director of a community recreation program, and directing the student activities program at a community college. After completing his doctorate he was on the faculty in the Department of Counseling and Human Development at the University of Georgia (1972–1978) and was coordinator of career counseling and associate professor of education at Duke University (1978–1980).

He has been active as an author and researcher, having contributed chapters to fifteen professional books and written over fifty articles for professional journals. Other professional contributions include over a hundred presentations to professional and other public audiences. He has been involved internationally with presentations in Europe and Asia and has publications that have been printed in Japan and Australia. Many of his topics on the concerns of college students and the changing nature of the college environment have been picked up as special stories by the media.

Over the past twenty years, Newton has served as a training consultant to students and staff in over forty college settings, including colleges in the United Kingdom and Japan. He has helped establish workshops and training programs in areas of leadership, organizational development, and peer counseling. He has been involved with the implementation of six grant programs sponsored by foundations and federal government programs.

Newton has been recognized for excellence in his teaching and service contributions to professional associations. In 1999 he received the Annuit Coeptis Award from the American College Personnel Association.

ATA U. KARIM is a licensed psychologist and coordinator of multicultural training and outreach at Kansas State University Counseling Services. He is also actively involved in teaching graduate and undergraduate courses. He received his doctorate in counseling psychology from Southern Illinois University at Carbondale in 1996. He received a master's degree in industrial and organizational psychology at California State University, Long Beach, in 1991. He was an international student from Pakistan when he came to the United States for higher education. He holds master's and bachelor's degrees in psychology from University of Karachi, Pakistan. He has received 320 hours of advanced training in intercultural communication issues and multicultural organizational development through the Summer Institute of Intercultural Communication.

SALLY LIPSKY is associate professor in the Learning Center Department at Indiana University of Pennsylvania. As coordinator of reading and study skills, she teaches developmental reading and freshman-year module courses. Additionally, she is supplemental instruction coordinator and participates in training and supervising peer educators. She has a Ph.D. in language communications from the University of Pittsburgh.

Peer Educators on the College Campus

Learning Objectives

After completing this chapter the peer educators will be able to

1. Explain to others the role of college students serving as peer educators.

2. List several helping positions on college campuses that are staffed by peer educators.

3. Understand and be able to employ an active process model of learning that includes three elements—sensing, personalizing, and acting.

4. Explain the importance of role modeling within the helping role.

5. Define the role of a mentor and assess their own ability to provide mentoring relationships with others.

The peer educator role is a valuable experience for most college students. For some it will last a year or two, for others it will chart new career objectives and lifelong personal change. In either case, we believe you will find the peer educator role to be both challenging and rewarding. If you take up one of the many peer educator positions open on modern college campuses, you will have the opportunity to make positive and in some cases significant differences in the lives of other students. We believe you will find the personal rewards of serving as a peer educator substantial—and the responsibilities as well. Additionally, we believe this training program and your subsequent experience as a helping person have the potential to have a very powerful impact on your own life, allowing you to explore and extend yourself to make the most of your own best qualities.

Exercise 1: You, the Helper

Describe why you have chosen to pursue a peer educator position on your campus. What personal characteristics do you possess that indicate that you are, or can be, a helping person?

_____

_____

_____

_____

Peer Educators

There are many terms used to describe student helper positions on a campus—peer educator, peer counselor, paraprofessional, mentor, student assistant, student educator, tutor, resident assistant, orientation leader, and many more. The authors have used the term *peer educator* as a comprehensive descriptor in this text even though many of the other terms describing peer or paraprofessional duties are synonymous and you may find them used in an essentially interchangeable manner in other sources.

Here is a working definition of paraprofessional peer educators that encompasses many campus roles and provides a starting point for the development of training skills and competencies:

Paraprofessionals are students who have been selected and trained to offer educational services to their peers.

These services are intentionally designed to assist in the   ✳
adjustment, satisfaction, and persistence of students toward attainment of their educational goals. Students performing in paraprofessional roles are usually compensated
in some manner for their services and are supervised by
qualified professionals [Ender, 1983, p. 324].

These terms have several common characteristics as they are used
throughout the literature regarding college students' serving in helping roles. As the words imply, *educators* assist others in the learning
process, *helpers* assist others in an array of activities, and *paraprofessionals* are helpers with specialized but limited training that enables
them to perform specific tasks typically performed by professionals.
In your role as a peer educator, we expect that you will be assisting
others through educational activities that professionals around you
would be performing if you were not available. However, your appointment is not a stopgap or a cost-cutting measure—you are serving in this role because you have the capacity to be as effective as
your professional counterparts—and in some cases more effective—
at delivering some types of services while deriving substantial benefit for your own education. These services, cutting across a variety of
peer educator roles, include providing information, explaining pol-
icies and procedures, orienting new students, making referrals, offering specific help strategies for problem-related counseling issues,
implementing social and educational programs, enforcing rules, providing academic advising, facilitating community development,
assisting with study skills, offering tutoring, and providing crisis intervention services (Winston and Ender, 1988).

Brief Historical Background

The use of undergraduates in helping roles on college and university
campuses has a long and rich history. Students in residence halls have
served as resident assistants, proctors, hall counselors, and advisers
since the early 1900s (Powell, Pyler, Dickerson, and McClellan,
1969). Student tutors have been assisting their peers with forms of

academic assistance since the colonial period of American history (Materniak, 1984).

Over time, there have been two major shifts in the use of students as peer educators. First, there has been a substantial increase in the variety of positions now filled by peer educators. The change is significant, increasing from the more limited use of peers as tutors and resident assistants to the now extensive use of peer helpers campuswide in all major service and educational departments. For example, Carns, Carns, and Wright (1993) noted that in more recent years students are assisting other students beyond the residence hall setting to include academic departments, reading and study skills centers, career and counseling centers, financial aid offices, and even in social and religious centers. Winston and Ender (1988) also found peer educators in student unions, international student services, crisis centers, and judicial offices, and in some cases directly involved with evaluation and research efforts. A recent review of the use of undergraduates in peer assistance roles on college campuses concluded that 76 percent to 83 percent of all higher education institutions make some use of peer educators (Carns, Carns, and Wright, 1993). Generally, it was observed that the larger the institution, the higher the percentage of utilization.

The second observation of current trends notes the primary manner in which peer educators are working with students. There is a growing preference for assisting students in groups rather than the more traditional one-to-one individual approach. Peer educators commonly assist students in classrooms, seminars, support groups, living groups, and in other collective ways. Both of these observations have direct implications for how students receive training and supervision.

Exercise 2: Peer Educators on Your Campus

Identify the types of peer educator roles on your campus. In these roles, does helping occur with individuals, groups, or both individuals and groups?

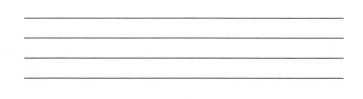

Peer Educator Effectiveness

Considerable research was conducted during the 1960s and 1970s that appraised the effectiveness of paraprofessional helpers. Much of this early study was the result of the Human Relations training movement, which identified and quantified the characteristics of an effective helper. These attributes include communications and relationship qualities such as empathy, respect, specificity, genuineness, and warmth—qualities, the researchers discovered, that could be enhanced through systematic training (Carkhuff, 1969; Carkhuff and Truax, 1965; Zunker and Brown, 1966; Brown, 1974). This training, although initially designed for professional preparation, was found to have nearly equivalent outcomes with paraprofessionals. Carkhuff and Truax found that paraprofessionals could be generally equivalent or only slightly less effective than professionals in providing therapeutic assistance in mental health settings. Zunker and Brown concluded that paraprofessional counselors were as effective as professional counselors in providing academic adjustment assistance to entering freshmen.

More recent research continues to conclude that peer educators serving as paraprofessionals can have a positive impact on their fellow students. A number of studies, cited in Carns, Carns, and Wright (1993), have clearly established the positive benefits resulting from peer counseling and peer advisement (Brenden, 1986; Frisz and Lane, 1987; Kramer and Hardy, 1985; Lonabocker, 1987; Russell and Skinkle, 1990; Russell and Thompson, 1987; Presser, Miller, and Rapin, 1984). Similarly, peer educators have been used with effective results when addressing current campus concerns as diverse as educational dissemination of information about AIDS (Burke, 1989), the improvement of cross-cultural communication (Berg and Wright-Buckley, 1988), the treatment of eating disorders (Lenihan and Kirk, 1990), and the enhancement of personal relationships (Waldo, 1989). Clearly, it has been established that peer educators are effective in a broad array of helping situations.

Personal Impact

Perhaps the most significant effect resulting from the experience of being a peer educator is the impact on the peer educator's own life. Program administrators—that is, those in charge of running peer educator programs—ranked the positive impact that the position had on the student paraprofessional as the highest reason for using peers, among a list of positive outcomes (Ender and Winston, 1984). As a peer educator, you can expect that one of the most important outcomes of this experience will be an enhancement of your own growth in both knowledge and personal attributes. As you help others solve problems, your ability to resolve complex issues increases. As you demonstrate empathy and compassion for others, your sense of emotional well-being is heightened. As you work to assist others, you will find your own sense of contribution and personal esteem will grow. It has been established that peer counselors will be affected in many positive ways including enhanced self-worth and interpersonal skill development (Yamauchi, 1986).

Impact on Others

You have several advantages when it comes to working with other students. One important factor will be the age similarity between yourself and the students you are assisting. It is well established that the influence of peer interactions is paramount during the late adolescent and early adult years as one achieves greater independence from the role of authority. There are very positive benefits attained by observation of the action of another person who has gone through similar challenges and experiences. In many cases people learn best by having role models who can demonstrate productive ways to act in a common situation. Finally, as a peer you can bring energy, excitement, and freshness to any important helping situation on campus because of the newness of the experience to you and the challenge inherent in doing a good job. This is not to say that professionals could not bring similar characteristics to the position, but long use tends to make professionals' responses to the job less intense than those of people for whom it is new.

Distinguishing Between Peers and Professionals

The terms *adjustment, satisfaction,* and *persistence* help us focus on the educational role of the peer educator as contrasted with the professional roles of teaching and counseling. Peer educators help others through functions such as assisting, coaching, tutoring, and supporting rather than the professional roles of teaching, training, interpreting, and counseling. These contrasting terms are significant and they provide the major elements of distinction between the roles of peer and professional educators. One important aspect of your training will be to learn where the level of your competence to assist others ends and where the knowledge and skills of the professional must take over to provide the optimal learning experience for another student. We will cover the important distinction of determining personal boundaries and limits of peer service as well as the skills for making appropriate referrals in Chapter Nine.

Exercise 3: Peer Educator Versus Professional Responsibilities

What are the primary differences in the type of assistance you are going to provide to other students, and the assistance given to students in your sponsoring agency by your professional counterparts?

_____

_____

The Training Paradigm

There are three key components to training: knowledge, skills, and personal integration. As a part of your preparation to become a peer educator you will need to work on all three areas, the chapters of this text will address each of them.

Knowledge includes the major concepts that will be useful in your conceptualization and understanding of the helping function. The core knowledge base for helping others combines elements of psychology, sociology, cultural anthropology, and education. Specifically, in this text you will be provided with some basic concepts of human development, interpersonal communication, cultural indoctrination, group process, and learning theory.

However, even with a base of knowledge about any subject, you must have sufficient *skills* to communicate successfully and work productively with others. Some of these skills include the ability to listen, communicate accurately, show intercultural sensitivity, apply problem-solving strategies, lead groups, assess environments, and make referrals. You will be introduced to various strategies and methods to act successfully as a peer educator.

Finally, the most important variable in the helping process is you yourself! The most significant ingredients of effectiveness are *personal qualities* that include such features as self-awareness, accurate self-concept, confidence, commitment to others, motivation, and warmth. We will emphasize that a crucial part of being a peer educator is being a role model. Throughout the book you will be given opportunities to look at yourself and find ways to grow and improve as an example to others. The goal of a good role model is not perfection but openness to being genuinely human and willing to understand and develop oneself.

A Process and Reflection Model

The combination of knowledge, skills, and personal integration acquired in this training may best be accomplished through a process and reflection model of learning. Borton (1970) described this model by use of the terms *what, so what,* and *now what.* The Borton approach gives one a systematic strategy to use when processing new material, and it asks the learner to define the relevance of this new knowledge from a personal perspective. The definitions of the three stages follow:

1. *What?* This process concerns the sensing out of differences between your original reaction, the actual effect it has upon you, and the intended effect. For example, you could ask yourself, "What is the difference between the intended impact of the material or information and my reaction to it?"

2. *So What?* This is the transforming stage, whereby the learner must translate the new material or knowledge into personally relevant patterns of meaning. You may ask yourself, "So what value does this information have for understanding my own life or my work with others?"

3. *Now What?* This is the action stage of the process model. Here, the learner must decide how to act on the knowledge and apply the alternatives identified to other situations. You may ask yourself, "Now what am I going to do with this information?"

Using the Model

There are two different ways of applying the what, so what, now what sequence of thinking about new material (Ender, Saunders-McCaffrey, and Miller, 1979). One involves the analytical mode, which can be characterized as hard-driving, pointed, sharp, logical, tough, and rigorous. This method is reserved for the classroom training sessions and will be employed through discussion, role-plays, and other appropriate learning situations involving groups of people.

The second is more contemplative and reflective in nature. This is a more relaxed approach and one you can apply when you process the information after reading a chapter or sections of chapters.

———————

Reflection Point 1

Reviewing the themes of this chapter from the what, so what, now what process perspective, you would ask questions such as the following:

———————————————————

———————————————————

What did you think your training as a peer educator would entail? Do you find that there were major differences between your expectations of training and the information you have covered in this chapter?

———————————————————

———————————————————

So what do these differences mean to you? (Assuming there were any.) What implications do the expectations and reality of training have for you to enter fully and enthusiastically into this training experience? (We suspect that training, as we define it in this text, is much more thorough and complex than what you envisioned when you accepted your peer educator role. In fact, we expect you are experiencing some anxiety over the difference between what you expected and the reality presented here.)

———————————————————

———————————————————

Now what are you going to do to work through this dissonance if it exists?

———————————————————

———————————————————

———————

This process sequence is very appropriate for examining oneself in relation to new thoughts and ideas, personality characteristics, or intellectual areas—even the study of topics such as science or math (Ender, Saunders-McCaffrey, and Miller, 1979). Scientific experiments constitute a continuous cycle of inquiry that follows almost exactly the same progression—observing data, building interpretations, applying the interpretations, and checking the results. It is critically important to keep in mind that the material you will learn in this book will ask you to look at yourself and your own functioning as a human being. You will be a role model to the others you are helping. Your level of functioning will have direct impact on those with whom you work. It is very important that you know yourself and model the attributes of building on strengths and recognizing and working on weaknesses.

Training Assumptions

This training program is based on several assumptions (adapted from Ender, Saunders-McCaffrey, and Miller, 1979) designed to help you derive maximum benefit from it, and to enhance the impact the role of serving as a peer educator will have on you personally. These assumptions are important for you and your trainer to consider as you enter the program, because they will lead you to more positive and long-lasting results when you share them and act on them. If you just go through the motions, you won't get nearly as much out of the program!

Learning Is an Active Process

Learning, especially skill development, is not a passive enterprise. To fully benefit from this training experience, you must be an active participant. The principle that one must demonstrate commitment to personal growth and development if change is to occur applies just as much to peer educators as to the students who may be receiving assistance. Additionally, you must also bring commitment and energy to become a successful learner.

We encourage you to be an active learner in three distinct ways. First, through the use of the what, so what, now what model you are encouraged to employ a more reflective, thoughtful, introspective learning style as you read the training chapters. The reflective model of learning is designed to assist you with this process. Second, embedded within many of the training chapters are exercises designed to assist you as you think about new information and apply this information to yourself, your interactions with others, and the environment around you. These exercises will be assigned by your trainer. The third method of active learning occurs during the training sessions. Along with being thoughtful, we hope you will take risks in your thinking, be challenged to hear and often accept thoughts different from your own, actively participate in role-plays and other simulations, and truly enjoy the acquisition of new skills through feedback and practice. The more you put yourself into this experience, the more learning will occur.

Peer Educators Are Self-Aware

You are entering a position that will require you to encourage others to make changes in some way. This may involve acquiring knowledge, shifting behavior, developing a different way of valuing an experience, engaging in more effective group activity, or finding ways of developing greater self-responsibility. If any of these changes are to occur with the students you are assisting, the students must show some awareness of their present behavior and make some commitment to change. The same is true with you. If you are not aware of your level of functioning in the area targeted for change with the student you are helping, it will be difficult for you to model the appropriate behavior—and difficult for you to advocate a change strategy with the student seeking assistance. We will challenge you throughout this book to become more aware of who you are as a person and a student. You are encouraged to incorporate change strategies into your own life when areas of improvement are warranted. This provides credibility for what you are promoting as well as modeling the process for others. If you are unwilling to make a personal adjustment it will be difficult for you to challenge others to take the risks necessary to promote change in their life. As a helping person you must be genuine and congruent with who you are as a person and what you advocate for others when promoting healthy, self-directed, and self-responsible behavior.

Training Takes Place in a Supportive Community

For change to occur, the support of others is usually critical. In this training experience, you are of course responsible for your own learning, but you are also responsible for supporting others in their learning experience. By this we mean you should always try to encourage fellow students to take risks in their thinking, share their ideas, and practice new skills—in other words, you should support their attempts to master this new material. There is no place in training for talking down to others, assuming an authoritative attitude or demeanor, or making critical judgments about the worthiness of others' ideas and opinions. In fact, the opposite style has been found to be most successful in training: show support for others, provide encouragement to take risks, look for the positive rather than the negative qualities in others, and give feedback in constructive ways. When all members of the training community embrace these concepts, there is a greater opportunity for mutual benefit.

Training Requires Time, Practice, and Feedback

As you will be exposed to new content areas and be required to develop specific skills to help others, this training program should ideally occur over a series of weeks throughout a quarter or semester. You will need time to consider and reflect on new ideas, learn new ways of viewing the helping relationship, try out new ways of behaving as a peer educator, and master new skills. In some instances, to be truly effective, you will have to change your behavior or way of thinking. Long-term change does not occur overnight. It takes time to integrate new behaviors with new thoughts. You cannot fully integrate new behaviors without practicing those new behaviors. All this takes time.

The Trainer Is Your Role Model

As you advance through this training experience, look to your trainer as your role model. Just as you will be a role model to others, the person leading this experience is a model for you, and will exemplify the helping skills you are here to learn. We believe everyone leads best by example. We trust that this old adage will manifest itself in your training experience.

Peer Educators as Role Models

Most people understand the folly of the parent who says, "Do as I say, not as do!" Learning is most likely to be accomplished when there is consistency between the instructional message and the behavior of the person providing that message. You will be most effective as a helping person if you provide a positive role model and thereby make it possible that you will become a significant person, a mentor, in the life of other students.

Role Modeling

Consider a role model who has made a difference in your life and ask yourself the following question: Have I ever told this significant person about the important role they play in my life? If you are like most people, more often than not, significant others will not know that they are admired, observed, and even being emulated by you. People become role models because they are available for observation and have a special position of authority or are perceived as holding special qualities. Parents, older siblings, teachers, friends, leaders of organizations, or even those in the public limelight will often become role models. As a peer educator you will be in a position to be a role model for other students on campus.

Exercise 4: Role Model Characteristics

Identify a role model in your life. What personal or professional characteristics does this person exhibit that you attempt to emulate?

_____

_____

_____

_____

Your institution will be entrusting you with a position that carries important duties and serves in many ways as a representative of the college. Such a position engenders some immediate respect and admiration from others because you are expected to be responsible and accountable in helping other students. Thus other students will look to your words and actions for guidance and leadership in regard to their own behavior. They may even try to emulate you in certain ways. Will the behaviors they emulate support positive qualities that show responsibility and respect, promote growth, and enhance their educational success?

For example, if you are a study skills instructor, do you practice successful classroom and study techniques in your own academic subjects? If you are a peer health educator, do you practice safe sex? Practice responsible drinking? Balance your life with exercise and good nutrition? If you are a resident assistant, do you model respectful and cooperative community living? In summary, do you model through your values, attitudes, and behavior a lifestyle that is compatible with the goals of your peer educator role? This is an important point to ponder for yourself, because you can count on the fact that students you work with will be observing your actions.

———————

Reflection Point 2

Think about being a peer educator:

What behaviors describe a successful role model in the area served by your peer educator role?

_____

_____

_____

So what are the differences between those behaviors and your own behavior?

_____

_____

_____

Now what are some actions you can take to become a better role model for other students?

_____

_____

_____

———————

On Being a Mentor

Being a mentor is a special and trusting role in which one person, the more knowing, is in a position to assist another person, the less knowing. The area of knowing may only be in a specific facet of campus life, and in many other ways you will be considered a peer or equal. Nonetheless, being a mentor carries a commitment of time and attention to a person who wants to make improvements in their life. As a mentor, you will have a variety of ways in which you will encounter your partner (the person you are mentoring). These may include offering suggestions, modeling behavior, providing support, and even making gentle challenges that will nudge the person to make necessary changes. It should be carefully noted that in forming a mentoring relationship the point is not to create dependency but to promote self-responsibility, not to decide for someone but to encourage self-direction. A mentor may serve as a catalyst for change— but when a goal is achieved or a skill accomplished the partner must be able to own the achievement as their own.

Tips for Successful Mentoring

1. Make a personal commitment to be involved with your partner for an extended period of time. Successful mentors have a genuine desire to be part of other people's lives, to help them through the tough decisions, to see them become the best they can be. Mentors must be invested in the mentoring relationship for the long haul; they have to be there long enough to make a difference.

2. Respect individuals and their abilities and their right to make their own choices in their life. Mentors can not bring the attitude to the relationship that their own ways are better or that participants need to be rescued. Mentors who convey a sense of respect and equal dignity in the relationship win the trust of their partners and the privilege of being mentors for them.

3. Listen and accept different points of view. Most people can find someone who will give advice or express opinions. It is much harder to find someone who will suspend judgment and really listen. Mentors often help simply by listening, asking thoughtful questions, and giving participants an opportunity to explore their own thoughts with a minimum of interference. When people feel accepted, they are more likely to ask for and respond to good ideas.

4. Appreciate your partners' struggles and feel with them without feeling pity for them. Even without having had the same life experiences, successful mentors can empathize with their partners' feelings and personal problems.

5. Look for solutions and opportunities as well as barriers. A mentor balances a realistic respect for the real and serious problems that partners face with an optimism about finding equally realistic solutions. Mentors are able to make sense of a jumble of issues and point out sensible alternatives.

6. Stay flexible and open. Successful mentors recognize that relationships take time, and they willingly take the time to get to know their partners, to learn new things that are important to their partners, even to be changed themselves by the relationship.

Many of the qualities reflected in these tips will be explored as part of your training in later chapters of this text. Chapter Three will help you gain understanding of cultural differences and your responses to them. Chapter Four will help you enhance your listening and empathizing skills. And Chapter Five will help you broaden your problem-solving skills and strategies. The key point of mentoring is to understand that it takes a real personal commitment to enter into a relationship of this nature, and this commitment should be considered carefully as a condition of taking on a peer educator's responsibility.

———————

Reflection Point 3

Think about mentoring:

What are some of the skills and competencies necessary for developing a successful mentoring relationship?

———————————————————

———————————————————

———————————————————

So what are your present strengths and weaknesses in
these areas?

_____

_____

_____

Now what are some specific targets of your training, as
outlined in this text, that will be important for you to
master to be a successful mentor for another student?

_____

_____

_____

_____

Summary

Chapter One has provided you with an overview of the use of students in peer educator roles on college and university campuses. In
particular, the chapter focused on the historical expansion of undergraduates' serving in helping roles, the types of positions typically
filled by peer educators, and the effectiveness that can be expected
in these positions. In this chapter you have also learned what a peer
educator is and what a peer educator can do. We have distinguished
between those types of activities more appropriate for peer educator
paraprofessionals as contrasted with those best offered by professional helpers.

The chapter has also outlined the three components of a learning
process: knowledge, skills, and personal integration. Basic assumptions
of peer educator training were provided as well as a method you can
use to think about new information and reflect upon the manner that
this can be useful to your own situation and your work as a peer educator. Because we strongly believe that people serving in helping positions are role models of effective living, you were challenged in this
chapter to consider your present level of effectiveness as a student role

model, identifying your strengths and developing action plans to focus on areas that may need improvement.

Regardless of the specific role you will assume on your campus, it is important to note that you are joining tens of thousands of other students serving as peer educators across the country. You, along with them, have the potential to make a major and positive difference in the lives of fellow students. Enter into this training program with a commitment to be the very best you can be. Think seriously about role modeling and the mentoring relationship. Take risks to learn and be supportive of fellow trainees. Be positive rather than negative, supportive rather than judgmental, and active rather than passive. Training is a journey to new and exciting thoughts, ideas, opinions, and skills. Enjoy the trip!

Chapter One: Summary Questions

1. In your own words, define the roles of students serving as peer educators.

   _____

   _____

   _____

2. Name several campus roles occupied by peer educators.

   _____

   _____

   _____

3. Describe Borton's process model. What does he mean by sensing, personalizing, and acting?

   _____

   _____

   _____

4. Why are peer educators role models for other students on campus?

_____

_____

_____

5. What is a mentor? List five qualities of a successful mentoring relationship.

_____

_____

_____

_____

2

Student Maturation and the Impact of Peers

Learning Objectives

After completing this chapter the peer educators will be able to

1. Define key terms related to the maturation process including *growth, development, maturation, change, crisis, challenge,* and *dissonance.*

2. Describe five principles that commonly operate in the human maturation process.

3. Explain the personal, social, and contextual factors that influence the nature of change and personal development in the college environment.

4. Describe several examples of personal and academic challenges experienced by college students.

5. Understand several of the personal and academic challenges they have experienced or are experiencing.

6. Identify several environmental conditions that have a positive impact on student development.

7. Use strategies that can facilitate changes in students leading to positive growth and development.

It is natural and expected that people make significant changes as they grow and develop throughout life. In particular, students in the traditional college age group, those from about seventeen to twenty-five years of age, make many changes in how they think, how they feel, what they believe, what they value, and how they act in the world. Pascarella and Terenzini (1991), after completing an exhaustive review of research on college students from the late 1960s through the 1980s, noted that there are innumerable ways in which students change and college influences these changes.

This can be readily noticed by reflecting upon the people you have known as a college student. How have they changed? Students come to college and try out new perspectives and different behaviors. For example, you may know students who acted out and became party animals, who got religion and joined a church group, or who changed academic majors from science to business or vice versa, turned in their backpacks for briefcases, or found a group of new friends and decided to live together in a communal apartment. The list can go on indefinitely. But what is change? When are these shifts in life values and lifestyles normal and predictable? How and why do people alter the way they are? When is change perceived as growth to a higher level of existence and when is it decay or at least an impediment to reaching a higher level of existence?

Reflection Point 1

Reflect on the ways that you have changed since beginning your college experience:

What are examples of changes you have made? Consider changes in your behavior, habits, attitudes, goals, or relationships with others.

_____

_____

_____

So what do you believe influenced or helped to shape these changes for you?

_____

_____

_____

Now what do you think the changes you have identified, and the influences that created those changes, indicate about how college has affected your development?

_____

_____

_____

_____

Your Own Change and Growth

Developing an understanding of this process of personal growth and change will be useful to you both as a growing student and as a peer educator. As defined in Chapter One, your role as a peer educator is to provide service that assists others in their "adjustment, satisfaction, and persistence toward attainment" of their own educational goals. As an effective peer educator you can be an excellent role model just by allowing others to see the way you approach the choices, challenges, and opportunities that shape your life. However, in addition to demonstrating successful growth, you can take an active role if you become familiar with ways to assist other students as they deal with the adjustments and hurdles that are a part of the challenge all students face in reaching their goals. Knowledge of the principles of how human growth occurs and the factors that influence change—and those that characterize a supportive environment—can help prepare you to carry out your role more effectively. Considering specific examples of the challenges that are typical of college students will help you react smoothly and constructively to them the first time you encounter them in your new assignment. The information that follows in this chapter will not make you an expert, but it will give you a sufficient understanding of human development to help you make appropriate responses and strategies for students going through predictable periods of change.

Definitions

The meaning of a few key terms will serve as a starting point for your understanding of human maturation and the process of personal development and change. Several key words describe some of the basic concepts to be discussed in this chapter. These words are *change, development, growth, crisis, challenge,* and *dissonance.* The definitions follow:

> *Change* refers to alterations that occur over time in student thinking, feeling, and doing. Change can be qualitative or quantitative, progressive or regressive (Pascarella and Terenzini, 1991).
>
> *Development* describes a series of changes that people typically experience over the course of a lifetime (Stevens-Long, 1984).
>
> *Growth* implies the presumption of a progressive direction as one moves toward maturity with greater complexity, differentiation, and integration (Pascarella and Terenzini, 1991).
>
> *Maturation* implies the movement is occurring toward the next higher level of development. It is accomplished by drawing upon the experiences of the past and the ability to adapt to demands of the future.
>
> *Crisis,* according to Erikson (1963), describes periods when a person faces an important decision point—a need to choose among alternative courses of action that can be progressive, regressive, or neutral in terms of changing level. The manifestation of a crisis through an event, decision moment, or particular concern is reflected in this book by the word *challenge.*

A *challenge* may occur in one or more areas of personal and social life. A challenge arises from new or changing circumstances combined with concurrent reactions in the internal world (thoughts, feelings, attitudes, reactions) of the individual.

Dissonance refers to an experience of discomfort and anxiety when the status quo is disrupted. The feelings associated with dissonance become precipitators of change as the individual seeks to resolve or avoid the anxiety and alleviate the distress.

Five Principles to Guide Your Work

Five principles of human development are worthy of your consideration and should help you in your work with others (Miller and Prince, 1977; Ender, Saunders-McCaffrey, and Miller, 1979). Underlying these principles is the assumption that all students with whom you have contact will be in the process of resolving challenges that when successfully resolved will result in increased personal maturation. A review of these principles will give you some insights as to how you can assist others as they resolve various life challenges.

PRINCIPLE 1: Human growth and development occurs as a result of pressure from the environment, as a function of biological maturation, and as a result of the personal values and aspirations of the individual.

The impetus for change originates in many places. A new environment can create considerable anxiety for some people. That is why many peer educators will be involved with orientation or freshmen year experience programs that help students adjust to campus life. Others will work in health and fitness centers and will encounter students who may have various levels of fitness and body image concerns that cause them to focus on dietary or exercise strategies. Many college students may be exposed to new and expanding ranges of values and information that create a tension to redefine personal viewpoints.

College environments and the readiness of students to experience new possibilities for themselves will lead to a period of life in which the potential for change is at a high point. This period of potential change can be experienced as a very healthy dissonance when the student is open to entertaining new ideas and willing to take risks, try out new behavior, and listen to alternative—sometimes conflicting—points of view. A peer educator can play a supportive role in the weighing of options, the scrutiny of personal values, and the problem-solving decision process for choosing a new direction even when the student engaged in the effort is approaching the challenge cheerfully and without undue stress. On the other hand, students may also experience the dissonance of change in some potentially unhealthy ways. For example, students may have extreme emotional reactions, becoming angry and confrontational, experimenting with excessive and personally destructive drug and alcohol use, showing reckless and unsociable behaviors, or withdrawing and avoiding contact with others. A peer educator such as a resident assistant might play a significant role in providing and enforcing safe boundaries for students to live within reasonable social rules and understand consequences of breaking these boundaries. A peer educator may also be part of the support network that can identify when a person is struggling with the challenges of the college situation and needs the intervention and assistance of a campus resource or authority. At that point it is recommended that the peer educator seek consultation and potential assistance from or referral to a more experienced professional.

PRINCIPLE 2: The maturation process can be characterized by gradual changes and by various types of crises.

Normal development for most people is not a series of traumatic events but rather a continuous process of subtle and not-so-subtle challenges that creates a tension, a psychological dissonance, that pushes for resolution. Most are quite predictable and normal. People's lives, for the most part, unfold in similar ways. Perhaps the major difference among individuals is the level of personal competence that has previously been developed in the area of concern. For example, you and your peers on campus are all students, but some are better academically than others are. A new college environment presents the challenge of finding out which classes you are best prepared to take, developing the autonomy to make it to class on your own, organizing your study times and approach, and finding the resources such as library, computer center, or tutors in a timely way. A new student may be strong in knowing how to take notes but weak in being assertive and finding ways to seek out assistance. Entering a new college environment presents a similar challenge to all students in that each individual must learn how to manage and adjust to the academic expectations. For some students this is a very natural and easy progression, for others it may precipitate a much greater crisis.

In the peer educator role you will be working, for the most part, with individuals and groups of individuals who are experiencing this gradual change process leading to more effective ways of dealing with the world around them and developing their own maturity. From time to time, you will run into individuals—and in some cases groups of individuals—who are experiencing these changes at a critical level and are finding it difficult to make the adjustments. Many times this crisis is manifesting itself because the individual did not master tasks earlier in life that would have provided the necessary skills to cope with the present challenge. For example, if a person has never spent time away from home, or has never been away without experiencing homesickness (even for a night or weekend), coming to a residential campus may be a very traumatic experience, causing considerable dissonance for the new student in the residence hall. If, through your assistance and the assistance of others, this same person learns to adjust and feel comfortable in this setting, they will have mastered a developmental task that will be essential for later adult autonomy.

PRINCIPLE 3: Maturation is a cumulative process, and it is therefore necessary to progress successfully through simple developmental learning tasks before being able to complete more complex ones.

This principle first manifests itself in very young children, for example, when they are learning to talk. Initially, a child makes sounds that are an incomprehensible babble, then begins to babble the sort of sounds heard from other people. Then the child slowly begins to verbalize a few words and finally starts to speak in sentences. A child who does not speak words clearly by age two will find it quite difficult to form whole sentences. This, in turn will make it difficult for that child to express needs and simple communication, which will necessitate more dependency on the parent to take care of the child until the difficulty is resolved. Similarly, a college student who is still very dependent upon a parent to make decisions and take responsibility for individual tasks, from waking up in the morning to washing clothes, may be at a loss when it comes to coping with these responsibilities alone.

This is a principle that will have considerable influence in your work. In your peer educator role, you may be assisting others who must make adjustment through finding resources, making individual decisions, and establishing personal habits. To be successful, students must discover what they need to know and what information-gathering or problem-solving strategies are necessary for goal completion. Finding the correct starting point is critical for later success. Since the mastery of necessary skills for dealing with the present situation is predicated on past learning it is important to help the student identify any necessary, and sometimes remedial, learning steps that must be completed to meet a present demand. The key to locating a successful starting point is finding the place where an individual can stretch to new heights but not collapse under the strain of an unconquerable challenge. Assisting someone as they develop the series of steps they must take to reach goal completion is a critical role for the peer educator. Learning how to help others assess their present skills in the area under investigation is the key to determining where to begin in regard to resolving a present threat to psychological equilibrium.

PRINCIPLE 4: Individuals develop at somewhat different rates, and each person has a unique way of adapting to personal challenges.

The key to this principle is the concept of individuality. What works for you in regard to solving a particular problem may not work for someone else. Peer educators in helping roles can take nothing for granted and make no assumptions about another's ability to resolve the current challenge in their life. Even though everyone moves through life stages at similar ages and faces corresponding personal challenges, each one takes this journey as an individual—with individual problem-solving skills and strategies. As a peer educator it is extremely important to show respect and understanding for differences in readiness, experience, and aspiration.

PRINCIPLE 5: In each phase of maturation, an individual must acquire or master certain skills, knowledge, or behaviors that correspond with that phase.

The skills, knowledge, and behaviors required at each phase are an outgrowth of positively resolving the personal and intellectual challenges embedded in earlier phases of life. Traditional-age college students who successfully resolve the challenges they encounter at college are better able to address the challenges that will occur in later adulthood. Knowledge of the challenges that will face those you assist in your peer educator role will enhance your ability to provide effective assistance. Chickering and Reisser (1993) have outlined seven vectors of change that are the most common areas of challenge for the maturing college student:

1. Developing a sense of personal competence in the physical, intellectual, and interpersonal realms.

2. Managing emotions effectively—developing tolerance of others, handling loneliness, dealing with conflict, and handling strong feelings such as anger, depression, hurt, fear, desire, or anxiety.

3. Becoming more autonomous and learning to think and act on one's own; becoming less dependent on others while learning to act cooperatively with people in more interdependent ways.

4. Establishing an identity that defines one's self and presents this publicly in a unique but clear way. Identity includes an amalgam of other vectors of development (emotions, purpose, relationships, physical appearance, and competency).

5. Freeing interpersonal relationships to interact with others with tolerance and respect and develop the capacity for intimacy.

6. Developing a sense of purpose and philosophy of life that identifies clear goals and lays out the groundwork for choosing one's future including lifestyle and career.

7. Living with integrity so that one has an understanding of key values and beliefs that become blueprints for personal choice and provide a congruence between belief and behavior.

Variables That Influence Change and Development

Several factors play a role in the process of change for college students. Some of these variables are conditions that individuals bring with them to college. Every student has a fund of experience, a base of knowledge, and a repertoire of skills already in place. Each student also comes from a history of socialization with family, schools, churches, and friends that have shaped a set of values and beliefs as well as a pattern of acting upon the world. It has often been said that if you want to know what someone is going to be, look at who they are and how they presently act.

Development that will occur in the future rests heavily on attitudes, behavior, and accomplishments of the past that are actualized in the present. Outstanding college football teams recruit the best players from high school programs; academic admissions programs also look for probable high-achievers based on ability and achievement records before college. Although these preexisting conditions are important to consider when one assesses change in college, it is more interesting to consider what happens in college to influence change. The factors that follow are selected from some of the research conducted by Astin (1993) and the summary of research by Pascarella and Terenzini (1991).

The single most important variable on how much the college experience will affect a student is the student's level of involvement with college programs and activities. Astin (1993) found that the more students are involved with campus life the more they will be influenced by this engagement to learn and shape their lives. Therefore factors such as living on campus, working on campus, joining campus organizations, participating in activities, and relating to other college students will play a major role in the impact college has on the individual. Engagement is a two-way street; it requires intention and effort by the students coupled with opportunity and invitation from the people and agencies of the institution.

Societal conditioning and sometimes biological differences play a role as well, influencing which issues and what level of impact a challenge area may have on any given individual. For example, Gilligan (1982)—and other theorists viewing development from a female perspective—notes that women are more sensitive to their environment in terms of relationships, are affected more by relationship crises, and are more expressive of their feelings. Likewise, it is clear that people raised in various cultures will not have the same reactions to any given situation because of differences in the way each culture predisposes people to view the area of concern. The impact of cultural differences will be discussed in more detail in Chapter Three.

During the college transition period, when people move from their family of origin but have not yet entered the post-college world, the peer group is the most significant source of influence (Feldman and Newcomb, 1970). The peer group provides a source of support, becoming the predominant socializing agent during the college years. The peer group influences behavior by establishing norms for how to act (from the clothes students wear to the "in" places students hang out). The peer group becomes the major source for gratification and validation by the inclusion, acceptance, and recognition offered by fellow students. Because of the important reliance on peers during these formative years, peer educators can be particularly influential as models and mentors to other students.

The opportunities provided by the institution through its organization, programs, faculty, and staff can have a significant effect upon each student. A college or university determines its direction by its philosophy and mission, and—more important—through the organizational activity that carries out that mission. Physical resources such as libraries, computer labs, and tutorial centers influence intellectual development; recreation centers, intramural fields, health centers, and natural parks can influence physical well-being; cultural events and activity clubs available on a campus influence students' social and interpersonal development. However, beyond the bricks and mortar and beyond the formal organizations, the most important factor is the quality and frequency of interaction among the faculty, staff, and students of the institution. Peer educators can play a significant role in assisting students to make connections through information sharing and referral for all members of the campus community.

The compatibility and congruence of the overall institution environment (size, philosophy, curriculum, people) with the individual student will influence the potential for impact and change. People who feel different, out of sync, or misplaced in the college situation may stay detached, unaffected, and potentially fade away or drop out without having much opportunity for growth to occur. By contrast, people who believe they are in a compatible situation will tend to be more comfortable and attached to their environment. However, it should be noted that it is still important to have a degree of challenge and dissonance that can nudge a person toward expansion and growth. The balance between support and challenge is critical in the change process.

Exercise 1: Balance Between Congruence and Dissonance

Review the variables just discussed concerning the factors that can affect student change. Now choose one factor such as influence of peers, impact of gender difference, or involvement level with campus activity and personalize this factor to your own life. Do this by taking a blank sheet of paper and drawing a circle in the middle to represent yourself. In the circle draw symbols or use descriptor words to represent how you would best illustrate the way you view yourself on the particular dimension (for example, the type of activity and involvement you have with campus life, or your identification from a cultural or gender perspective). Now around your circle draw some additional circles representing your impression of other students (these can represent individuals or groups of students) and use descriptors or symbols to represent how you perceive them to be on the same dimensions. Now compare yourself to the impressions you have of others in your college environment. Note the amount of congruence and the amount of dissonance you may experience by being similar to or different from the norm of the campus. How does the congruence or dissonance affect you?

Developmental Challenges Confronting College Students

The upcoming sections outline several examples of typical developmental challenges confronted by college students in a number of key areas. These are situations, decisions, or tasks that need to be resolved and accomplished through a set of circumstances presented to the student. The student in turn will experience a level of tension, described as dissonance, until that challenge has been resolved. The discussion starts with the personal and academic challenges that face the entering student and progresses to the types of challenges that adult students may face while participating in a college program.

As a peer educator, you are not expected to have a comprehensive knowledge of all theories of human growth and development, but you do need some concept of the types of personal, social, and intellectual challenges that students typically experience as they grow and mature in college. This book will give you a good start. If you feel the need for a more in-depth exploration of student development theory you may wish to read further from Chickering and Reisser (1993) or an overview of developmental theories by Evans (1996).

Personal Adjustment Challenges

When students enter college they face a series of challenges created by entering a new environment and taking on a new set of responsibilities. The situation caused by adjustment to a new environment will vary for each student and may depend considerably upon the nature and familiarity of the environment. However, all students will confront a series of issues that will provoke reactions and challenges that need to be dealt with—and responded to—for a successful transition into college. These challenges may seem as simple as being responsible for waking up and going to class in the morning, but can also become much more complex as a student must learn to live comfortably with different people under new circumstances.

Take the hypothetical example of Sally Smith. Sally is an only child who has lived most of her life in one community surrounded by a secure group of friends and family. She has her own spacious room at home and has a very set pattern of family rituals and responsibilities (like when the family eats dinner, who takes care of household chores, and what time she is expected to be home on the weekends). She arrives at college and moves in to a dormitory room (about half the size of her room at home) that she shares with a roommate she has never met before. The roommate seems nice enough, but it is soon apparent that the roommate has different tastes on how the room is decorated and maintained. The roommate also has a boyfriend who spends quite a bit of time in the room without much consideration for Sally's privacy. Sally has morning classes and needs to get up by at least 7 A.M.; her roommate has later classes and likes to stay up to late hours.

It is clear that Sally is up against a series of critical issues that create dissonance for her and demand major adjustments. Emotionally, she misses her old family and friends but is excited about her new contacts and opportunities. She feels the tensions and conflicts of dealing with another person in a very limited physical space and yet wants to find ways to get along and become friends with a person from a very different background. Her values are challenged on a number of fronts as she makes decisions about the people, the activities, and the lifestyle that she will now lead.

Here are some examples of challenges typical to entering college students:

Physically moving to a new environment

Living with a roommate

Leaving parents, siblings, other supportive loved ones and friends

Living with people from other ethnic and minority groups

Taking the initiative to meet new and different people

Making personal decisions on a daily basis

Confronting noisy neighbors on the residence hall floor

Determining specific social groups to join

Facing peer pressure to consume drugs and alcohol

Facing peer pressure to conform to new ways of behaving that may conflict with personal values and beliefs

Intellectual and Academic Challenges

Most college students will face a series of choices and need to make decisions about the nature and direction of their academic experience. Built into the typical college experience are critical moments that create dissonance—declaring a major, signing up for courses, receiving midterm grades, finding financial aid, overcoming a deficiency, recognizing the need to get help. Students must resolve many of these situations in a college academic environment by dealing with faculty, resource personnel, organizational structures, and rules of procedure that in many ways embody the assumption that the student is now responsible as an adult to anticipate every need and carry through with a response. Here are some examples of these challenges:

Speaking up in class and asking questions

Visiting professors outside class

Joining study groups

Managing heavy course demands and schedules

Completing difficult classes in areas where the student may be weak academically

Figuring out multiple choice exams that ask for the "best answer" from a series of good answers

Understanding the registration, drop-add, course withdrawal, and other administrative procedures

Obtaining a tutor

Accepting the importance of the "core curriculum"

Developing semester course schedules

Seeking assistance on campus when academic problems occur

Balancing academic and social life

Physical Challenges

Students emerging through the late teens and entering the young adulthood period are often concerned about their physical appearance, physical competence, and manual skills. These areas are important for developing a self-identity in which one feels assured about body image, is physically active and healthy, and has confidence in physical attractiveness to peers.

Take another hypothetical example, Sonny Anderson. Sonny was involved in many sports throughout his high school years, but when he reached college he realized he could not compete at this next level. He kept up with some sports at an intramural level and through occasional workouts on his own time. After two years of college, Sonny recognizes that he is not as active as he once was and has gained about twenty pounds and feels uneasy that his body is not as trim as he would like it to be. Part of this is due to not having the same regular sports to play, but Sonny knows that he eats a lot of fast foods because he doesn't like to cook for himself in his apartment. He also is drinking beer when he goes out and has started smoking cigarettes on these social occasions. Changing his lifestyle, dealing with new habits that are difficult to break, and maintaining the discipline to follow through with activities supportive of improved physical health are the issues now concerning Sonny. Sonny is not alone on the campus—the list that follows includes some examples of things many students deal with:

Coping with weight gain and loss

Learning to control diet and alcohol consumption

Competing athletically with other, more gifted students

Finding time to learn and implement physical exercise programs

Accepting one's body type and working within one's own limits

Forming positive health habits and learning how to break problem habits

Becoming self-reliant about managing stress, illness, or other health problems

Finding hobbies, avocations, and physical activities that can be maintained over a lifetime

Interpersonal Challenges

Relationships are a major concern of college students and an area that causes many students to experience stress and anxiety. Making and maintaining connections has a profound impact on a student's life. Students will evolve through different levels of relationship needs as they mature through their college years. During the initial entry into college the student may focus on finding a group to belong to and acquaintances to be engaged with in activities. Later, the relationship issue may evolve toward how to express and manage feelings, and how to share more personal reactions and receive support. As interactions grow, issues of relationship may become more complex and deeper—managing conflict or making meaningful commitments come to the forefront. Further examples of interpersonal challenges follow:

Connecting and becoming a part of a friendship group

Making and managing romantic relationships

Asserting oneself with others when personal rights are violated

Interacting with members of ethnically or otherwise different groups

Dealing with loss or separation from a significant relationship

Terminating relationships that are no longer positive or growth-enhancing

Tolerating the various forms of eccentric behavior demonstrated by significant others

Sharing personal information with close friends and loved ones

Being cooperative in group projects and activities

Learning to show emotions in appropriate ways

Experiencing the personal benefits of helping others

Accepting the responsibility of a committed relationship

Managing conflict situations

Being secure enough to say no to peer pressure

Recognizing sexual orientation and, for gay and lesbian students, deciding whether to "come out of the closet"

Career and Lifestyle Challenges

These challenges become more prominent as students move into the last couple of years of their college experience. During this time significant decision points occur that may have long-lasting consequences. These decisions can become major challenges for college students and can be accompanied by significant dissonance. Here are some examples:

Choosing an academic major

Changing an academic major

Deciding on appropriate internships, externships, and practicum experiences

Deciding to "stop out" or drop out of school

Making significant decisions regarding issues of marriage and coming to terms with income needs and the lifestyle consequences of this decision

Unique Challenges for Adult Students

Today, there is a significant increase in the number of adults returning to college to begin or complete a degree or to go through certificate programs or other types of continuing education experiences. Adults returning to school also experience many of the personal and academic challenges identified for traditional-age students. However, adult students may have several additional challenges in their life. For example, Gloria is a thirty-five-year-old woman who is the single mother of two children, six and nine years of age. Advancing her career through a college degree in business is a motivating long-term goal, but she will encounter many pressures and demands while getting this degree. Although taking charge of her children is a major responsibility, she must also hold a job to pay the bills—and would like to "have a life" with time for enjoying friends and maintaining normal activities. There are many adult students in college with equally challenging goals and responsibilities. Their challenges may include

> Managing multiple personal responsibilities—home, family, and work
>
> Adapting to the college learning environment and feeling confident with entering academic skills
>
> Changing directions in work and career
>
> Feeling comfortable in an environment that may be dominated by traditional-age students
>
> Finding and interacting with a supportive group of peers
>
> Developing course schedules that are compatible with other responsibilities
>
> Finding a place on campus to study, rest, and meet with friends
>
> Commuting to class and finding adequate parking
>
> Finding appropriate child care
>
> Finding sources of financial support

Reflection Point 2

Consider your present life situation as a college student:

What significant concern or challenge are you now experiencing in your personal maturation process?

_____

_____

_____

_____

So what human resources (peer educator–staffed programs) are available on your campus to assist you as you resolve this concern? Note: If you cannot identify a peer educator service on your campus that could be of assistance, what professionally staffed college department could assist you?

_____

_____

_____

_____

Now what action could you take to make use of a formal peer educator service or through an informal contact with peers?

_____

_____

_____

Exercise 2: Life Challenges and the Peer Educator

Think about the area in which you are preparing to become a peer educator. From the preceding list of personal, intellectual, physical, interpersonal, career, and adult challenges facing college students, identify the ones you might expect will most affect those seeking your assistance. Think of some additional examples of challenges or concerns common to students you may work with. Compare your ideas with those of others in your training group.

_____

_____

_____

_____

_____

_____

Conditions That Promote Student Development

There are certain conditions and characteristics of an environment that encourage and support an individual's movement through a period of transition and change. When you promote these conditions you improve your ability to assist students in dealing with a personal challenge that has created dissonance in their life. Miller and Prince (1977, p. 17) describe the qualities of an atmosphere that people will perceive as encouraging and supportive:

1. Freedom to risk disclosure of innermost thoughts and feelings without fear of attack or rejection

2. Being allowed to begin at one's own level, move at one's own pace, and master each succeeding level of learning before moving on through the developmental process

3. Having opportunities to identify emerging developmental needs and have an equal voice in deciding what learning to pursue and how to proceed

4. Being able to observe and interact with others who effectively model the characteristics, values, and processes that best represent the outcomes to which the environment is committed

5. Receiving accurate and usable cognitive and affective feedback and reinforcement in response to behavior

6. Having opportunities to practice and test out new ideas and actions

7. Being encouraged to learn increasingly complex behavior and apply it, as appropriate, to situations of daily life

Each of these seven characteristics has implications for peer educators who plan programs and interventions to assist other students in their growth process.

Tips for Implementing a Supportive Atmosphere

1. Take a genuine interest in the individual student's personal situation so that an atmosphere of support and care can be established that promotes awareness and exploration.

2. Stimulate the student to become aware of options and opportunities beyond the present status. Suggestion and nonthreatening forms of challenge can be impetus for the student to move to a higher level.

3. Provide avenues (people, places, activities) in which a student can explore the options and opportunities beyond the present situation.

4. When impasses and problems arise, demonstrate problem-resolution strategies to move the student toward solutions. These may be activities you apply yourself or by referral.

5. Help students assess where they are through the use of reflection and feedback.

6. Be proactive by providing programs and activities that anticipate the needs of students based upon what is known concerning developmental levels.

Exercise 3: Environmental Influence

Consider the educational environment of your campus.
Does this environment promote healthy student maturation? Support your answer by giving examples of campus
characteristics, programs, and individuals that promote
positive development. If your answer is no, what is the
campus lacking? What could you and other peer educators do about any deficits you have noted?

_____

_____

_____

_____

_____

Summary

This chapter has explored how students go through the process of
change that accompanies normal growth and development. For traditional-age students the college years provide a backdrop for a significant period of maturation into adulthood. For older students
college may represent some equally challenging transitions to be
mastered. The concepts and principles of maturation were summa-
rized and the factors that can affect development were discussed.
Variables that promote healthy human maturation were described
along with guidelines for how peer educators can have a positive
impact when working with students who are dealing with issues relevant to their growth and maturation.

The way change occurs and people mature is important for you to
consider as you successfully make your own transitions and as you prepare to understand this process in those you serve. Knowing the personal and academic challenges of students who seek your assistance
will provide you with a much stronger base of knowledge to be of

help. In some cases the help you can provide is to refer students to a service, resource, or more prepared professional helper.

***

Chapter Two: Summary Questions

1. Explain how the concepts of dissonance, crisis, and change are related to human maturation.

   _____

   _____

   _____

   _____

   _____

2. Review the list of developmental challenges in this chapter and determine the ones that are most likely to be affecting the students in the situation in which you will be assisting as a peer educator.

   _____

   _____

   _____

   _____

   _____

3. Explain how the variables such as involvement in college activity, gender identification, peer group behavior, and faculty interaction will influence the issues of development and change.

   _____

   _____

   _____

   _____

   _____

4. Examine the five principles universal to human maturation. Choose one and explain how that principle may affect your work in your peer educator role.

   _____

   _____

_____

_____

_____

5. In your role as a peer educator, how can you help create an environment that stimulates positive growth and development?

_____

_____

_____

_____

_____

3

Intercultural Competence

Ata U. Karim

Learning Objectives

After completing this chapter the peer educators will be able to

1. Define intercultural competence.

2. Define cultural programming.

3. Know the relationship between generalizing and stereotyping.

4. Identify forms of prejudice.

5. Recognize hindrances to intercultural competence.

6. Understand the four steps to genuine intercultural competence.

7. Understand and explain the influence of personal, social, and institutional factors on discrimination and prejudice.

8. Identify five propositions essential for intercultural success.

The changing demographics in this country point to a rapid diversification of the workplace in particular and society in general, and intercultural competence is therefore becoming an essential requirement if one is to manage human relations successfully. It is important for you to consider the frequency of your daily interactions and the diversity of the people with whom you interact.

Think about the last time that you spent an entire day on your campus without coming across someone who was different from yourself. In reality, changing demographics make it almost impossible to escape differences. Everyone encounters differences in gender, ethnicity, race, religion, sexual orientation, class, age, and ability, to name a few. A primary responsibility of a peer educator is to work competently and effectively with all members of the college population regardless of their group affiliation. A peer educator, therefore, must be comfortable working with diverse audiences. Regardless of your current personal comfort level in this area, you will find that intercultural competence is a skill that can be acquired or strengthened.

Intercultural Competence

The term *intercultural* is a useful substitute for the more commonly used *multicultural* and *diversity*. Its implications are broader than simply working with people from other cultures. *Subjective culture* (Triandis, 1972) is the amalgam of values, beliefs, and ways of looking at the world that people always carry within themselves. Group affiliations and living-learning environment heavily influence a person's subjective culture. Although each individual may share many culture-centered tendencies with culture-mates, the interpretation and understanding of these tendencies remains very personal. Remember that the concept of culture goes beyond arbitrary categories of geographical and racial-ethnic demarcation. People live in a larger culture that holds many subcultures. For instance, the students from a rural setting might have a culture different from that of urban students—even those who come from the same state.

In this chapter, *intercultural competence* is defined as the capacity of people to understand and interact effectively and successfully with others who differ in cultural beliefs, behaviors, values, and worldview. When people possess intercultural competence they have the skill to accept their own cultural programming, appreciate personal differences without making negative judgments, and refrain from indiscriminately applying stereotypical information and overgeneralizing secondhand information about groups to all members of those groups. They are able to process incoming information without exaggerated bias and discrimination. They recognize that their worldview is only one of many ways to understand and experience the world and that various concepts and functions may not have the same meaning across cultures.

Cultural Programming and Discrimination

There have been times when prejudice has been considered an evil manifestation of human nature. In reality there are more plausible explanations for the nature and function of prejudice. Prejudice provides important psychological functions for people (Brislin, 1993). The term *cultural programming* (Hofstede, 1991) is used to identify the various ways in which culture influences how people make sense of their situation, create a value and belief system, and develop a worldview. Individuals' positive and negative reactions to events, people, and other phenomena in their environment are the result of their cultural programming.

Cultural programming takes place over a lifetime. As people live and learn they develop a worldview that allows them to make sense of the surrounding world and to make decisions about their interactions in personal, communal, and institutional realms. This worldview allows them to operate almost automatically within a cultural context. They believe they know the appropriate way of being. This helps conserve time and energy in their daily activities.

Reflection Point 1

Think of a group that you typically view negatively:

What emotional, behavioral, or intellectual response do you typically have toward this group that is different from your response to your own group?

So what aspect of your past cultural programming do you believe has created this reaction?

_____

_____

_____

_____

Now what might be one step you could take to get more information about this group of people that might begin to change your present worldview?

_____

_____

_____

_____

———————

Generalizing and Stereotyping

To survive, it was important for the first humans to be able to make decisions about threatening events and act quickly to deal with the danger. Automatic responses are both easier and more time efficient. For instance, consider Grandpa caveman walking down the path and detecting a shadow. He had to make an instant determination whether the shadow was made by something he could eat or something that would eat him. He obviously did not have the time to contemplate matters in detail as he did not want to become caveman à la carte. So large, instantly available categories of information were necessary for him to make quick judgments. Surely he had quite a number of false alarms that made him jump and run. He probably even felt foolish later, but at least he survived. People continue to make similar instantaneous judgments based on easily accessed information about a variety of situations—including those posed by other people. The tendency to make generalizations based on global categories of information stems from the automatic nature of accessing this information. This information may or may not be true with regard to the situation or person at hand. Also, much of this information may be secondhand, stereotypical, or inaccurately generalized.

To illustrate this point, what is the first answer that comes to your mind when you think of the gender of people in the following professions: doctor, teacher, auto mechanic, librarian, nurse, and pilot? Did you respond male, female, male, female, female, male? Most people will. Despite the fact that they may actually know people in these professions who are the opposite gender to the answers typically given, people still tend to give answers are based on stereotypes or prototypes of gender. It just happens that information that is most reinforced and most easily accessed will jump to the forefront. There is nothing wrong with these responses. It is what is done with this information that is important. For instance, if people persist with their first response as accurate and true, they may have difficulties in interpersonal interactions and find themselves unable to work effectively with those who do not fit stereotypes of that given group.

Neutralizing Stereotypes

People can work to neutralize the impact and influence of secondhand information so that their reactions are consistent with the objective reality of a situation—not a subjective response based on information that is not correct for the event or person in question. Often, people tend to create categories of information that can be easily accessed when an event or person activates a specific category. The immediate or first response is usually based on the information that is available in that category. For instance, if you are of European American or Asian American descent, consider what passes through your mind when you pass an African American man on campus. If you have not had extensive personal interactions with African American men you will react to the information that is accessed in the category "black man." If that information is based on media portrayal of

African American men, the first information you access may include that they are angry and dangerous (based on the commonly available stereotypes) and, perhaps, you respond negatively or with some apprehension. If you are African American, substitute some other group for your thought experiment—most people have similar categories for various human groups, events, and experiences.

Prejudice

Brislin (1993) has outlined various functions of prejudice. Prejudice is a construct often used for serving the interests of groups and people. It allows people to feel good about themselves by judging others to be less. This includes such areas as moral, physical, intellectual, and emotional prejudice. Prejudice allows people to express their values and morals and defend them by claiming to be in the right, while seeing those who do not share their values and morals as being in the wrong. Religion, politics, and sexuality are good examples. Stereotyping is often used as factual information and is incorporated into individual decision making.

In addition to protecting self-image and speeding up decision making, prejudice also allows protection of one's group identity and way of life. The ability to clearly identify ingroup and outgroup members helps people look after and protect the interests of those who are similar to and least threatening to the established worldview and lifestyle preferred by the group. It is important to remember that while these functions have been identified separately, they are very much interrelated and interactional in nature. They combine their influence on the decision-making processes of the holder.

Prejudice may be manifested or expressed in many overt and covert ways, and it is important to know what these different types of discrimination include. This knowledge will help one find ways to reduce and hopefully—over a period of time and with ample practice—eliminate unwarranted prejudice toward outgroups and their members. Brislin (1993) has identified various types of discrimination and prejudice:

"Isms"

The obvious form of prejudice is overt, intense Isms. Isms include all forms of discrimination based on various group identities, such as racism, sexism, and ageism. These Isms may be based on cultural or religious beliefs and definitions of inferiority and superiority. They are used to identify outgroup members as being inferior on intellectual, physical, or moral dimensions, thereby dehumanizing them. Such dehumanization can be used as a rationalization for mistreatment.

Tokenism

Another form of prejudice may result from perceived interference of a group in the traditional way of life for the majority, or ingroup. Tokenism is another version of prejudice often prevalent at the institutional level, occurring when people look at particular outgroup members as receiving token accommodations particularly if there are legal requirements. For example, it is tokenism to hire someone from a minority group protected by law if the hiring is based on external criteria of equal opportunity and not on the qualifications of the applicant for the job. Tokenism may lead to the deliberate (though perhaps unacknowledged) selection of an unqualified candidate, so as to set up a self-fulfilling prophecy of failure and reinforce the prejudices of the person doing the hiring.

Armchair Discrimination

This type of discrimination includes selective interaction. For instance, someone may be comfortable and at ease working with a gay man in the office but may not feel comfortable with his presence in a social setting.

Symbolic Issues

This type of prejudice occurs when one group views another group as interfering with and threatening important cultural values. For example, cultural symbols such as locus of responsibility, work ethic, value of time, and attitude toward authority can lead people from various groups into direct conflict.

Real Conflict

People often find themselves in conflict over limited resources—money, jobs, political power, quality housing, schooling. When they perceive their competitors in terms of rival group identity, the conflict and the prejudices feed on each other and exacerbate both. In some cases it is so much more congenial to attribute a rival's success to group rather than individual factors that people invent and emphasize differences that they did not perceive as important or even existent until the conflict arose.

Reflection Point 2

Think of the ways you have seen prejudice exhibited on your campus:

What is the most noticeable type of prejudice that you see on your campus?

_____

_____

_____

So what are the implications of this prejudiced behavior for members of the oppressed group?

_____

_____

_____

Now what actions can members of your campus community consider to reduce or alleviate these acts of prejudiced behavior?

_____

_____

_____

Hindrances to Intercultural Competence

There are multiple hindrances and stumbling blocks to positive intercultural interaction (Paige, 1993). Many times these hindrances are interconnected, and it is important to recognize them both as individual factors and as they influence each other. In the beginning phase of initiating contact with someone who is significantly different from yourself in worldview and cultural programming it will be important for you to consider the obstacles described in this section.

Dealing with Personal Discomfort

Most people like to live in their comfort zones, preferring tranquility to anxiety. Being around familiar people and places reduces the anxiety level and lets people act and behave on autopilot. They assume that people who share their cultural reality will understand them without much difficulty. They know that they will behave in culturally appropriate ways with regard to eye contact, interpersonal distance, and communication style. People often feel uncomfortable in situations and with other people who are unfamiliar and are prone to act, and even think, differently in those situations. They are concerned about what are the appropriate behaviors. It is difficult to relax and be yourself in that sort of situation. Most people, if they had to choose, would associate with others just like themselves.

Fear of Ingroup Rejection

People tend to make sense of society and social environments in terms of their group identity. The idea of *us* and *them* is a very simple way of explaining the ingroup and outgroup phenomenon. *Us* constitutes the ingroup and *them* constitutes the outgroup. "What will my friends say—" is a thought that often interferes with intercultural interactions. This ingroup pressure to conform and stay loyal can lead to a strong fear of being abandoned or rejected by the ingroup if one continues to engage in outgroup socialization. Many people discontinue outgroup socialization at the first hint of ingroup displeasure.

Fear of Outgroup Rejection

"They won't want to have anything to do with me—" is a common response. People often feel that any attempt to interact with outgroup members will lead to rejection from that group because they may not want to "interact with us and have personal relationships with us" due to intergroup differences. This thought of rejection usually occurs during the beginning stages of relationship building. It is easier not to start intercultural relationships because of the hidden assumption of what will happen. The expectation of being rejected often interferes with intercultural interaction.

Fear of Loss of Identity

"I don't want to lose my values, morals, and identity—" One set of reservations that can hinder intercultural interactions stems from a fear of identity loss. People feel that they will change in an unacceptable way if they allow themselves to be exposed to other cultures. For instance, a person with strong traditional family values may mistakenly believe that interacting with and befriending gay and lesbian individuals will somehow destroy the established belief system and create a negative change.

Fear of Embarrassment

Engaging in new activities carries an inherent risk of embarrassment. Interactions in an unfamiliar or less familiar social context create the fear of inappropriate behavior's evoking derision from those who know the appropriate behaviors and manners. This self-consciousness may actually increase the perceived embarrassment because the person is trying to act perfectly in accordance with the appropriate rules of conduct.

Reflection Point 3

Think about your relations with people whose backgrounds differ from your own:

What hinders you most when exploring or interacting with members of other cultures or outgroups?

_____

_____

_____

So what are the implications for you when you allow these hindrances to block your personal growth in regard to meeting and interacting from others different from yourself?

_____

_____

_____

Now what could you do to take some personal risks and move beyond this hindrance that is blocking your intercultural relationships?

_____

_____

_____

_____

Developing Intercultural Competence

The discussion to this point has covered cultural programming, the nature and function of prejudice, and hindrances to intercultural competence. This section introduces a developmental learning model to improve your intercultural competence in the areas of cultural self-awareness and intergroup social relationships, and in regard to communal and institutional factors.

Learning Intercultural Competence

A developmental programming approach to acquire intercultural competence involves exploration, discovery, learning, and practice (EDLP). For lasting change in the area of intercultural competence to occur, it is important for people to go through the following steps:

exploration of their current intercultural development, *discovery* of variables that influence intercultural development, *learning* new or different skills to enhance intercultural development, and *practicing* or engaging in the newly learned skills to make them permanent. The EDLP model is based on the following assumptions:

- *Intercultural competence can be learned.* Anyone can increase their intercultural competence by receiving appropriate training and experience.

- *Intercultural learning is an experiential process.* One cannot become interculturally adept by only reading books. It is important that learning be through experience as well.

- *Intercultural learning is developmental.* Just as a child needs to learn to crawl before walking, so must people learn the initial skills for intercultural success before they attempt more advanced skills.

- *Change needs to be created in the thinking, feeling, behavior, and beliefs of the participants.* People are holistic, and do not think, feel, or behave in a disconnected fashion. Thoughts, feelings, and actions are interconnected.

- *Safe yet challenging learning environments facilitate progress.* People tend to be open to learning new and challenging tasks when they feel safe.

- *Intercultural learning requires an understanding of personal, social, communal, and institutional issues.* It is important to recognize how these four concepts are interlaced, and must therefore be explored and integrated into the learning process.

- *Change requires effort, some discomfort, and patience.* Intercultural learning and competency challenges people to grow in directions that may not come easily or comfortably.

- *Intercultural learning can be transforming.* It can open new doorways of understanding and perception that are not available to monocultural thinkers. It enables people to experience and interact with the world in a more complex manner, one that is both respectful and filled with wonder for differences.

Cultural Self-Awareness

People who do not see themselves as cultural beings have difficulty in processing any meaningful discussions that revolve around intercultural issues. It is difficult to understand and accept cultural explanations for human behavior until one is clearly cognizant in this area.

Exploration

The first step toward intercultural competence is getting to know yourself as a cultural being. Your judgments, beliefs, values, morals, opinions, attitudes, assumptions, and ways of looking at and making sense of the world—particularly with regard to interpersonal, communal, and institutional relations—and your interactions with other people are primarily cultural. Members of the majority culture may say that they have no culture. For instance, European Americans—particularly those who have lost touch with their ancestors' home countries—are frequently heard saying that they don't have a culture. In fact, they are swimming in culture, but do not recognize it due to its vastness and engulfing nature. They do not consider their clothes, food, music, art, architecture, and institutions as cultural manifestations. If the same people are put in another part of the world, or for that matter, in a different homogenous ethnic or racial neighborhood, they will instantly realize that not only do they have a cultural identity, they have one that is very important to them. By its very nature, cultural programming is very implicit, deeply embedded, and extremely experiential in nature.

Exercise 1: Cultural Programming

Consider an example of cultural programming, the perception of time. Pay attention to how you think about time. Is it a free-flowing entity, or is it something linear and very well defined? What is your cultural programming about time? What importance do you attach to punctuality, or to your time-telling instruments? How do you talk about time? Do you say things like "Don't waste my time—" "I don't have time—" "When the time is right—" "After a while—" or "In due time—"?

_____

_____

_____

_____

_____

Now use the same approach and think about your beliefs, opinions, values, and morals about some other important intercultural variables. For instance, what do you think about work ethic, personal responsibility, gender roles, and attitudes toward authority? This list is by no means exhaustive. As you consider these words and the personal meaning you attach to them, are you starting to see yourself as a cultural being? Are you identifying and acknowledging some patterns in the way you make sense of your world?

_____

_____

_____

_____

_____

Discovery

Through exploration, you can find out what you think and feel from a cultural perspective. It's also important to consider the process of how you got to be the way you are. The task in this area is to trace learning sources and their influence on you.

Exercise 2: On Time

Again, consider *time*. Answer the following questions to develop an understanding of what time means in this culture:

1. How does the culture talk about time? For in-stance, consider the various phrases associated with time. "Time is money—" "Come on—time's a wasting!" Can you think of some other phrases?

   _____

   _____

   _____

   _____

   _____

2. What are the cultural reminders of the importance of time? Think of the various time-telling devices in your house. Start with the obvious, a clock. Now think of all the other devices that tell time.

   _____

   _____

   _____

   _____

   _____

3. What do you think of people who are not punctual? Alternatively, what do you think about someone

who always insists on doing things exactly at the promised minute? Think of all the assumptions that jump to your mind about a person once the question of punctuality comes up.

_____

_____

_____

_____

_____

Learning

Cultural self-awareness requires one to look at things with a critical eye. For instance, the next time you order at a fast-food place, consider the symbolism attached to this activity. Think about the importance of time. Ordering takeout at a fast-food establishment saves a lot of time compared to preparing an elaborate meal in your kitchen. What about the importance of utilitarianism? Fast food is not the best-tasting food but is quickly available, quickly consumed, and the utensils and food holders are disposable. The drive-through window makes it even faster. The point is that the process of learning involves a deeper understanding and critical analysis of daily-life phenomena, phenomena that people normally take for granted.

This should begin to give you a clearer understanding of yourself as a cultural being. At the same time, it is important to remember that although there are broad commonalties in how people in your culture behave, perceive, and explain life, your perspective is unique. People carry their culture within them because they process and experience environmental events and social phenomena through the filters of their personality and personal experiences. Therefore, it is important not to believe that the opinions of an individual about their culture are an objective and accurate representation of their group as a whole. No one is an expert regarding their culture or their people. People can speak accurately only about themselves with regard to their personal experience and interpretation of their culture.

Practice

The primary purpose of practice is to solidify new skills so that they are easily accessible when needed. Practice will also increase your comfort with cultural exploration activities. Now that you have learned some strategies for cultural knowledge acquisition, you need to apply and practice what you have learned. This can be done simply by discussing the obvious with others from your culture, allowing you to develop a framework to discuss and understand cultural phenomena more accurately and quickly. With practice you can look and see the hidden lines and contours that are deeply embedded in cultural tendencies.

Reflection Point 4

Think about money:

What has your culture taught you about the personal significance you attach to money?

_____

_____

_____

So what significant issues arise between yourself and others because of the significance you attach to money?

_____

_____

_____

Now what can you communicate to others when these issues occur to help them understand your cultural background related to this area?

_____

_____

_____

_____

Intergroup Social Relations

Knowing yourself as a cultural being is the first step toward improving intercultural interactions. Even within a single culture, communications between two or more people can involve frequent misunderstandings. Every participant processes the information in a unique, personal manner—while assuming that all the others share that manner. In any intercultural interaction, there is an additional layer of cultural influence on information processing, and as the processing filters increase so does the probability of miscommunication.

In addition to communicating, people are also actively involved in reacting and responding at an emotional and intellectual level based on the available information relevant to the conversation partner. For instance, when men and women talk with each other they are not only engaged in processing the information passing between them but also making judgments and assumptions about the other gender based on generalizations, stereotypes, and other secondhand information available to them. Extended social and personal interaction with people from different cultural backgrounds can be an anxiety-provoking experience and creates intercultural fatigue and stress. This may well be one of the primary reasons that people do not eagerly engage in such interactions. Miscommunication is commonplace when people from different backgrounds interact.

Exploration

Use the same approach as for cultural self-awareness and pay attention to your immediate thoughts and feelings about people who do not share your cultural background. Do certain generalizations come up for you when you think about members of the opposite sex or other ethnicities, nationalities, religions, sexual orientations, education levels, economic levels, social status levels, and abilities? Pay particular attention to groups that you have difficulty relating to and interacting with, or understanding their way of life and worldview.

Exercise 3: Personal Reactions

To aid you in this analysis, fill in the following incomplete sentences with the first thoughts that come into your mind. Don't stop to work out politically correct answers. Remember, you are getting to know yourself as a cultural being and there is no better way than complete honesty with yourself. You do not have to share these feelings and thoughts with others.

Women are . . . _____

Men are . . . _____

African Americans are . . . _____

Whites are . . . _____

Poor people are . . . _____

Gays, lesbians, bisexuals are . . . _____

Discovery

Now that you know a little about what you think and feel about various groups of people, consider the process of how you came to these feelings and thoughts. The task in this area is to trace the learning sources and their influences on you. Take a category such as how you consider "poor people." Think of the messages that you received about poor people from parents, friends, religious teachings, the media, government sources, and teachers.

Think of any other information sources that are influential in your life. Identify them and the nature of the messages communicated by them. Did they verbally and nonverbally clearly communicate particular assumptions about poor people, their values, work ethic, or ethnicity? Or did they communicate their assumptions and beliefs more subtly through their personal interactions with poor people? Do they behave exactly the same with poor people as they do with those with more generous incomes? Consider your conclusions about people who are poor because of these messages.

Learning

Now that you know a little more about how and why you feel and think a certain way about various groups of people, are you open to changing or in some way altering your feelings and thoughts about these groups? If your answer is yes, you can move to the next step of gaining new skills to overcome current negative views and substituting or adding new information to modify your current knowledge and information. On the other hand, if your answer is no, it is important to explore your reasons for not wanting to expand in this area.

There are several strategies you can implement to alter your point of view about outgroups. The first step is to identify the factors with which you judge other groups. For instance, are you dismissing, ignoring, or uncomfortable with people because of their membership in a group? Do you find yourself saying, "I cannot get along with So-and-so because—" and finishing the thought with statements like *she is a woman, he is black, she is a lesbian,* or *he is a [member of some religion]*? This gross rejection of a group serves as a very unsophisticated way of sorting out relationships. It is high in prejudice but low in discriminatory value because the reasons for the discrimination are not well defined. Another level of discrimination is to reject people not on the basis of their group membership but on certain personal characteristics that are associated with the entire group (stereotype). For instance, "I cannot work with So-and-so because—" *she is too emotional, he is too lazy, she is not bright enough,* or *he is too sensitive*. Discrimination in this situation is now more defined and the prejudice becomes more covert. There is good rationalization for not wanting to engage with members of outgroups because they do not have the abilities and characteristics that you value. It is important to recognize that perceptions of out-group members typically grow out of actual firsthand evidence or secondhand information that colors your perceptions. In reality, you may be seeing someone as being emotional or lazy because of their group membership and not because they actually are exhibiting those characteristics.

This is called differential processing of information. For example, say that you like someone—you're apt to consider their little behavioral mannerisms cute. On the other hand, if you do not like a person exhibiting the same behavior you may perceive it in a less flattering light. Consider a time when you may have judged an out-group member differently from an ingroup member who displayed the same behavior. The skill that you need to develop is to focus on monitoring your information processing. You will need to pay attention to how you are reacting to the information about an individual based on words and actions. Being more intentional about how you process information, particularly when outgroup members are involved, is very important.

Differential Criteria

Everyone has a tendency to use different criteria for assessing satisfactory competence or success when it comes to outgroup members. For example, people in an outgroup get held to a higher standard of performance than those who belong to the ingroup. Think about your own associates from other cultures. Are you assessing and measuring them by how close they are to your way of behaving? Do you reject and accept on the basis of difference and similarity rather than a more complicated, contextually based criterion of judgment that accounts for cultural biases? To be contextual in your information-processing skills, you need to maintain a constant awareness of your cultural biases or inclinations and develop your skills of active listening and accurate observation.

Personal Dialogue

This technique will help reduce first-impulse reactions to outgroup members and differences of opinion. Based on your initial emotional reaction, you must ask yourself the following question: What is it in the presentation of the person or message that makes me react negatively? The emphasis is placed on what you are hearing and not what the person is saying. Many times people hear messages differently and the impact of the communication is very different from the intent of the communicator. As you find answers to your questions you will begin to recognize patterns of reactions that occur for you with different outgroups. Then the reactions are evaluated for appropriateness for the given context within which they are occurring.

Strengthening Contradictory Information

Another important and challenging task is to create strong links and access to information that you have received that contradicts existing stereotypical or secondhand information. Your intention must be to remember and revisit contradictory information that is more accurate, comparing it with inaccurate information and attempting to replace the latter. Many people have a tendency to remember and accept information that complements their beliefs and reject information that contradicts those beliefs that have been internalized.

Reflection Point 5

Think about gender relations:

What immediate negative thoughts do you have when you think about members of the opposite sex?

_____

_____

_____

_____

So what negative thoughts can be generalized to all members of the opposite sex?

_____

_____

_____

_____

Now what can you do to stop generalizing in this manner?

_____

_____

_____

_____

_____

Practice

This one is easy. Pay attention to the information that you are receiving every day. Determine if you actively and easily agree with information that reinforces old beliefs and assumptions about outgroup members. For example, take the statement, "foreigners are sneaky." In this case, if you only pay attention and reinforce this belief when you come across foreigners who confirm this opinion or belief, you may ignore foreigners who are not sneaky and dismiss this information as an exception to the rule. Monitor how you pay attention to information that contradicts the internalized belief system about outgroup members. Also pay attention to how you feel about specific outgroups. Now attempt to discuss these feelings in a safe environment with others who may have struggled with the same issues. You may want to gather more accurate information about the outgroups by actively pursuing accurate informational sources, such as members from that group. Asking members of your ingroup who are more positively disposed toward the outgroup in question may also prove useful.

Communal and Institutional Factors

Everyone belongs to specific communities and institutions. A community differs from a social group. It tends to have more contexts and may have many relationships between its members that are not social in nature. One example is a residential neighborhood. It is made up of many people and while all may not have close interpersonal relationships they have some communal relations. Similarly, institutions tend to be large organizations that are in place to serve some formal purpose in society; for example, the school you are attending. Communal and institutional factors play an important part in intergroup relations. This is particularly true when considering ingroup and outgroup interactions. Issues of social justice, acceptance, appreciation, and equity for others regardless of their identity group are influenced by institutional factors.

To prosper in the modern world, people must begin to look at themselves not only as independent individuals but as integral members and participants in their community and institutions and thus in the larger cultural system. This is crucial because issues of power and privilege exist within the communal and institutional context and cannot be discussed or understood without understanding one's membership and contribution to the communal and institutional systems.

Exercise 4: The Influence of Communities and Institutions

Consider the following questions to discover how communities and institutions influence both your behavior and your worldview, attempting to keep the status quo.

1. What is the definition of success and status at your college?

   _____

   _____

   _____

2. What kinds of behaviors are rewarded and pun-
   ished at your college?

   _____

   _____

   _____

3. What are the characteristics of the leaders at your
   college?

   _____

   _____

   _____

   _____

4. What are the characteristics of ingroup members at
   your college?

   _____

   _____

   _____

   _____

5. What are the typical privileges of being a member
   of your college?

   _____

   _____

   _____

   _____

6. What methods are used to discourage outgroup en-
   croachment into your college?

   _____

   _____

   _____

   _____

Communities and institutions fulfill various functions in the
larger cultural system, including gatekeeping, declaring values, and
defining the worldviews of their members.

Gatekeeping

Gatekeeping is a social process that makes sure that people who enter communities and institutions are not a threat to the equilibrium that already exists. When change is introduced into a system, conditions emerge that require accommodation. Systems, like humans, do not like change and tend to resist it. It is important to remember that sociocultural systems share the common tendency of systems to strive for equilibrium. Institutions serve to protect and ensure such equilibrium even when it comes at the expense of outgroups. Many times gatekeeping occurs with members of minority groups. It is important to understand that equilibrium and the status quo based on inequity is not stable, even if the illusion of stability exists. As conditions of difference increase in intensity, attempts to maintain equilibrium and status quo can become the catalyst for system disruptions. In these situations chaos may be a necessary phenomenon to accommodate the needs and rights of the outgroup members.

Role Formation and Evaluation

Anyone who enters a community or an institution is expected to fulfill certain roles within particular context and culture. This helps organize people into certain manageable categories that to some extent put boundaries on the expected behaviors, thereby increasing the predictability and lowering the probability of chaos and conflict in the system. It also allows the system to reward and punish its members.

Social Structures

Institutions and communities are usually responsible for outlining desirable and undesirable social behaviors and tasks resulting in the formation of social structures. Systemic values attached to certain behaviors make them mainstream or marginal. Rewarded behaviors tend to strengthen the dominant and traditional value systems in place. For example, military personnel are expected to follow orders.

If you are involved in a religious organization there may be certain behavioral and value expectations and an organizational hierarchy to follow.

Strengthening Ingroup Privilege

Ingroup members usually have greater ease of access to systemic resources and upward mobility in the hierarchy of power. They also tend to find themselves in a safer living environment than outgroup members may experience in the same system.

Exercise 5: Cultural Valuing

Answer the following questions:

1. Do you question the current dominant culture value system's impact on outgroup members?

   _____

   _____

   _____

2. Can you identify the reward system of the dominant culture within which you reside? Is it applied fairly to all members of the system, both ingroup and outgroup members?

   _____

   _____

   _____

3. Identify five privileges that you experience as an ingroup member of your community.

   _____

   _____

   _____

   _____

   _____

4. Do you understand how your community and various systemic institutions influence the outgroup members' quality of life on a daily basis?

_____

_____

_____

5. Discuss with an outgroup member their experience of living in the same system. How does it differ from your experience as an ingroup member?

_____

_____

_____

_____

Intercultural Success

The following five principles are essential for intercultural success.

PRINCIPLE 1: All assumptions are cultural.

People are cultural beings heavily influenced by the general cultural tendencies to view the world and judge it in specific ways that they have learned over a lifetime, implicitly and explicitly. They tend to consider their own view as the right, the only, and the absolute way of experiencing and processing the world around them. This assumption may lead to errors of inference and attribution that interfere with an accurate processing of information that violates standard expectations of communication, behavior, and values.

PRINCIPLE 2: It is necessary to suspend judgment temporarily.

While it is not possible and would be very anxiety-provoking to suspend judgment indefinitely, it is possible to suspend the immediate judgment of an event or person temporarily, while gathering more firsthand information to formulate a more accurate judgment. This is particularly important in situations where the immediate judgment is based on inaccurate, generalized information or stereotypes.

PRINCIPLE 3: Context and content both matter.

Many times people judge others only on the basis of limited information. Because intercultural situations are not necessarily functionally or conceptually equivalent, it is easy to make mistakes in understanding familiar behaviors and communication that may have had a different function or concept in the other person's culture. It is therefore useful to pay attention to the context in which the behavior is occurring, as well as to the actual behavior. This yields a better understanding of the event or behavior in question because it is processed against the contextual backdrop. For example, you might consider a group of people to be angry and hostile by how they behave. If you limit yourself to just the observable behavior and current situation you limit your understanding of why this group is acting as it is. Hostility and anger become the content to which you respond. On the other hand, if you know the reasons for this behavior, you have the information about the context within which the behavior occurs. This may give you the opportunity to react more accurately because you now have the bigger picture.

PRINCIPLE 4: Becoming comfortable with discomfort is both possible and necessary.

Becoming comfortable with situations that cause an anxiety response will be beneficial in intercultural relations. The ability to stay engaged in an interaction despite some discomfort can lead to reduction of discomfort through practice. This is more accurate for situations where the intercultural interaction is positive. Another important function of this area is to help you grow as a person. Developmental growth emerges out of some discomfort or dissonance, and the resolution of that discomfort promotes growth. Shrinking away from such situations and staying well within established comfort zones only maintains the status quo. Intercultural growth employs the same developmental principles that were discussed in Chapter Two. As the discomfort is resolved, the probability to benefit from and enjoy intercultural interaction and expand one's ingroup definition increases.

PRINCIPLE 5: Curiosity and deliberate inquisitiveness improve information accuracy.

This principle facilitates intercultural discovery. The more curious and inquisitive you are, the more accurate information gathering becomes. It also allows you to be a critical consumer and intentional collector of information and knowledge. Practice facilitates the inquiry process and encourages better and more sophisticated methods of information gathering. This also helps you challenge an existing belief system, which is apt to be based on secondhand information. You will be able to make firsthand decisions about people and events that will be more accurate, because they will be based on information you gathered for yourself.

Summary

Intercultural competence is a skill that can be learned. It is developmental in nature and very experiential; developmental in the sense that you must develop or have certain existing skills before moving on to the next level of learning, and experiential because intercultural competence will come with doing. For example, you can not learn to be a better speaker, athlete, driver, or cook without practice. The same is true for learning and internalizing intercultural skills. If you were only to read books (including this chapter), you would never develop greater competency in this area.

You now have a better understanding of how you experience, process, and respond to the world around you. If you stopped here, you would have awareness of your worldview and the reasons for why you are the way you are. Nevertheless, you still would not know what to do about it. The learning phase involves the changing of current unintentional ways of reacting and becoming more intentional in how you process your experiences. You begin to learn better ways of processing information that allow you to be more accurate in your conclusions. The next step is to test this information firsthand, by examining the weight you attach to secondhand information from sources other than yourself.

Chapter Three: Summary Questions

1. In your own words, define the role of culture in influencing your worldview.

   _____

   _____

   _____

2. Name the different types of risks involved in intercultural inter-actions.

   _____

   _____

   _____

3. Describe the different types of prejudice.

   _____

   _____

   _____

4. What are the five keys to intercultural success?

   _____

   _____

   _____

5. Name and describe the steps of the developmental programming approach discussed in the chapter.

_____

_____

_____

6. Describe several ways of understanding and critically analyzing the personal and interpersonal involvement of people in regard to understanding issues of diversity.

_____

_____

_____

_____

4

Interpersonal Communication Skills
Creating the Helping Interaction

Learning Objectives

After completing this chapter the peer educators will be able to

1. Describe the differences between ordinary, daily conversations and the special qualities of interpersonal communication that are necessary for an effective helping relationship.

2. Articulate several reasons why advice giving is not the appropriate response in the context of most helping interactions.

3. Demonstrate the ability to communicate core conditions of helping, including empathy, respect, and warmth.

4. Demonstrate effective attending skills in the helping interaction.

5. Demonstrate appropriate listening and responding skills so that other students can explore their own problems.

6. Demonstrate the ability to communicate interchangeable responses in a helping interaction.

7. Describe four types of situations they may encounter in the helping relationship that mandate a referral to another helping person with more advanced training.

Many times in your role as a peer educator, you will be called upon by other students to assist them as they explore and resolve problems associated with the personal and academic challenges they experience as college students. In some instances, these problems will be clear-cut—the student will need some necessary information or action from you. For instance, a student in a residential setting may need some assistance in understanding a housing policy such as a contract. This type of request for help requires you to respond with direct information. Or students seeking career guidance may need you to introduce them to the career development office or show them where it is located. This is a request for action on your part. These types of requests for information or action are typically straightforward, requiring little helping expertise in the area of interpersonal communication.

By contrast, the types of helping requests that this chapter will address are the ones where students seek you out for your understanding and involvement (Gazda and others, 1977). These situations typically require high levels of proficiency in communication because the students may describe personal dilemmas that are not clear-cut, easily identifiable, or quickly solvable. The students may be experiencing emotions such as confusion or anxiety in regard to the problem presented. They are clearly experiencing personal distress and are seeking your understanding and involvement to assist them in clarifying the problem and identifying strategies for resolving it.

This request for understanding and involvement requires verbal and nonverbal responses from you that differ dramatically from your responses to requests for direct action or information. In these instances, you are being asked to enter into an interpersonal relationship with the student, focusing on issues that require the student to explore the issues causing the psychological dissonance. In your helping role, your interpersonal communication skills will aid the student in the self-exploration process and will help lead the student to greater levels of personal understanding, culminating in action or problem-solving. In other words, your job is to help the student solve the problems, not to solve them yourself.

Advice Versus Interpersonal Communication

Many peer educators may at first find it difficult to apply the interpersonal strategies suggested in this chapter to improve their communication in a helping relationship. This is the result of a lifetime of experience and practice in a quite different form of day-to-day helping—advice giving. For the most part, advice giving looks like the appropriate response when friends, family, and coworkers share their problems and concerns. In fact, this is what many people ask for and seem to expect, and in daily life it often really is appropriate. However, several problems associated with this helping strategy make it a less effective tool for peer educators who are assisting others with interpersonal problems and concerns.

Advice Giving Is Easy

Giving advice is a relatively simple act. A person describes the problem and you immediately give your best take on the situation. No problem exploration has occurred and, in fact, you will never know if the initial problem that is presented is the real problem that needs to be addressed. For instance, a student complaining about a roommate's actions will not benefit from your advice if, in fact, the real problem is hesitancy to confront the roommate rather than what the roommate is doing. Perhaps this same student has difficulty dealing with most interpersonal relationships when conflict arises, and this "problem with the roommate" is really only a symptom of a greater issue. You might never address the real problem of conflict avoidance if you provide a one-minute sound bite of advice about the specific situation the student described. Instead, you need to learn how to draw out the underlying concerns—which the student may well not have recognized—and provide support while the student works out ways to deal with them. This is apt to be a new way for you to help other people and may take some getting used to, but is a very useful skill to master.

The Helper Is the Expert

When people give advice, they are thinking and responding from a personal frame of reference: values, attitudes, past experiences, and present maturation level. Unfortunately, the recipient of the advice must operate from a completely different set of personal values, attitudes, past experiences, and developmental level. What works for one person may not work for another person at all. The principle to follow is to recognize that the person seeking assistance is the expert regarding himself or herself. The action to be followed must be consistent with who they are as a person, what they value and believe in, and the choice they are willing to live with in their own life.

Advice Giving Involves Little Time Commitment

A person who is in real need of your understanding and personal involvement needs a commitment of time from you. Problem exploration, self-understanding, and the identification of problem-solving strategies are not to be dealt with in a few minutes of conversation. The skills recommended in this chapter would require a willingness to spend some time with another student if successful problem resolution is to have an opportunity to occur.

Advice Giving Is a Low-Energy Activity

Advice giving does not involve much personal or emotional energy on the giver's part. You can quickly gather data, sort it through your personal frame of reference, and come up with a solution. Effective interpersonal communication, on the other hand, requires appropriate attending, listening, and responding skills within the other person's frame of reference. In other words, problem resolution occurs best when the person helped is at the center of the exploration process. You will learn that this requires quite a bit of concentration to focus your attention on another person and, as the saying goes, "walk a mile in their shoes." Effective helping is a high-energy and at times intense activity. You may experience some feelings of fatigue after a successful helping interview with another student, and you will probably feel somewhat tired mentally and perhaps emotionally.

Advice Giving Requires Little or No Skill Development

Advice-givers bring their present maturation level, past life experiences, values, attitudes, and beliefs to the helping interaction. They filter their thinking through these personal dimensions and give advice. On the other hand, effective interpersonal helpers have developed several specific helping skills. These include understanding how people mature and develop; attending and listening effectively; demonstrating and communicating empathy, respect, warmth, and genuineness in the helping interaction; and implementing a problem-solving model. These are all specific skills that can be learned, practiced, and implemented.

Advice Giving Demonstrates a Lack of Respect for the Individual Seeking Help

Advice-givers respond completely from their own frame of reference, taking all the responsibility for the outcome of the problem being addressed. This, in fact, shows a lack of respect for the other person's ability to resolve the problem in a manner consistent with who they are as an individual. Also, if the solutions suggested do not work, the person who sought assistance has little or no personal responsibility for the lack of success. They can say, "I just did what I was told was best." By contrast, effective helping through interpersonal relationships promotes independence, not dependency. Effective helpers trust that others have the necessary human resources to discover and implement solutions to their problems, and act as guides along the path of exploration, understanding, and problem resolution.

Advice-Givers Have No Limitations

As advice-givers are presumed to be experts, there may be no limitations to the problems they hear or the advice they propound. However, helpers practicing from the interpersonal skills model should be willing to identify both their strengths and their shortcomings when working with others in a problem-solving relationship. They will be able to discriminate among the problems they are hearing, understanding when they may be of assistance and when it will be necessary to refer the student to someone with more sophisticated helping skills.

Reflection Point 1

Think about communications:

What are the major differences between advice giving and effective interpersonal communication?

_____

_____

_____

So what will be the major changes you will have to make in order to change from an advice-giver to one who practices effective interpersonal communication?

_____

_____

_____

Now what must you do to move toward greater effectiveness?

_____

_____

_____

Characteristics of a Helping Relationship

If effective helping is not giving good advice, what is it? How will you know if your interactions with others are helpful? What are the differences between ordinary, day-to-day conversations and those that can be described as helpful within the context of effective interpersonal communications? There are ten characteristics that can be used to distinguish between helping relationships and relationships that may not benefit those seeking help. The following characteristics and brief summaries have been adapted from the work of Shertzer and Stone (1974) by Ender, Saunders-McCaffrey, and Miller (1979, pp. 51–53).

The Helping Relationship Is Meaningful

Both participants value the helping relationship between them. At times, it can be both personal and intense. It is meaningful because it is relevant. It may be both anxiety-evoking and anxiety-reducing, involving mutual commitment between the peer educator and the student seeking assistance.

The Helping Relationship Involves Feelings

In true helping relationships both parties tend to disclose those parts of themselves that are creating anxiety or dissonance. This self-disclosure may produce many feelings for both the peer educator and the person being helped. Even though intellectual factors are certainly operative and valued, the feeling domain is revealed and discussed in the helping relationship.

The Helping Relationship Reflects Personal Integrity

The self-worth of an individual is respected in the helping relationship. Shame, pretension, and deceit are not present in a relationship built on respect for a person's self-worth. Both individuals relate to one another as authentic, reliable human beings.

The Helping Relationship Takes Place by Mutual Consent

One cannot truly be helped if the interaction is based on coercion. The absence of pressure is a vital element in the helping relationship. Both parties should enter the relationship free of external pressure. This is a critical characteristic if genuine help is to be given and received.

The Helping Relationship Involves Communication and Interaction

In the helping relationship both parties convey, exchange, transfer, and impart knowledge, information, and feelings. This information is exchanged both verbally and nonverbally. The more lucid and articulate the communication between peer educator and student, the more meaningful the relationship.

The Helping Relationship Shows a Clear Structure

Even though the degree of structure will differ depending on the relationship, there are two essential patterns present—stimulus and response. Responsibility for this structure is placed on both parties. In the beginning stages of the relationship the peer educator will be required to initiate and at times explain the process of the helping relationship. As the relationship develops, however, the student will learn to take part more fully.

The Helping Relationship Is a Collaborative Effort

Both participants in the helping relationship work toward a mutually agreed-upon goal. Both seek out resources and contributions that will be additive in a partnership, moving toward goal achievement.

The Helping Relationship Is Designed to Produce Change

The significant element here is that the person seeking help will be somehow different after receiving the help. This difference, if the relationship was helpful, will be defined in positive ways by both the peer educator and the student.

The Individual Seeks Understanding and Involvement

Although there may be many different reasons for seeking assistance, the student assumes the peer educator can, in fact, be of some assistance in resolving the problem causing concern. It is crucial to the relationship that the student has confidence that the helper can be of meaningful assistance.

The Peer Educator Is Approachable and Secure as a Person

Effective peer educators develop a manner that encourages others to seek them out for help. Their behavior is accepting of others and respectful of people in general. Peer educators need to free themselves from undue doubt, anxiety, and fear, which may create barriers to approachability.

Reflection Point 2

Think about the ten characteristics of a helping relationship:

What are the ones that seem most natural to you given your present style of helping?

_____

_____

_____

So what characteristics may be difficult for you to presently model or implement?

_____

_____

_____

Now what can you do to integrate some of these more difficult characteristics into your helping style?

_____

_____

_____

Effective Interpersonal Communication: Components of the Model

The type of helping described within this area of effective interpersonal communication draws its theoretical base from Human Relations Training (Egan, 1975; Carkhuff, 1969; Gazda and others, 1977). These trainers of paraprofessional counselors were also researchers who have successfully proved that people with limited amounts of helping skills training can be effective when assisting others as they sort through, clarify, and resolve life problems that are interfering with day-to-day functioning.

To be effective in this helping role, peer educators must learn and demonstrate appropriate attending skills, active listening techniques, empathy, and interchangeable responses. Also, peer educators using this model must be able to remain nonjudgmental in regard to the problem they are hearing and must genuinely desire to assist the student seeking their help. All these positive components of helping must occur within a relationship framework that can be categorized as having high levels of trust, respect, and warmth.

Attention Skills

Paying attention to another person when engaged in interpersonal communication in a helping relationship involves two dimensions—physical attending and psychological attending.

Physical Attending

Demonstrating appropriate physical attending skills involves focusing completely on the individual seeking help. Your body should be communicating nonverbally that you are really tuned in and interested in the person as they seek to clarify their problem. You will probably be sitting down, making good eye contact, and providing supportive expressions of warmth and caring. You will not be displaying behaviors that may be distracting to the person seeking help—no fidgeting, distracting body movements, or judgmental facial expressions.

Psychological Attending

Psychological attending is your ability to focus on the whole person and their feelings, thoughts, and intentions, while expressing your attention through your active listening and responding skills. Here you are focusing on both the verbal and nonverbal messages the student is sending. You will be determining if they are consistent or congruent. You will be absorbed in the communication and willing to attend to the nuances of what the person expresses. You will be tuning in to such variables as the person's tone of voice, facial expressions, posture, animation, silences, pauses, and gestures. Everything is important. Psychological attending involves truly trying to enter into the other person's world, seeing and experiencing the world as they do. This will demand substantial concentration and energy from you.

Two other important psychological dimensions of helping are demonstrated through appropriate attending skills. These are respect and warmth. *Respect* is the belief in the capacity of the people seeking help to help themselves and can usually be demonstrated by good attending behavior, refraining from doing anything for people that they could do for themselves, and supporting people in their efforts (Gazda and others, 1977). *Warmth* is primarily communicated through nonverbal signals, which may include a touch or hug, or a smile or other facial expression.

———

Exercise 1: Comfort Zones

With a partner in your training group, sit facing each other. Experiment with the concept of physical distance and its relationship to comfort and warmth. How do you feel when you sit one foot apart? Ten feet apart? Three feet apart? Notice the physical mannerisms that you and others in your training group use. What nonverbal messages may be communicated to another person through

your physical mannerisms? Your trainer may ask you to
share your thoughts with others in your group.

_____

_____

_____

_____

_____

_____

Listening Skills

One test that indicates whether a helper is listening intently to the
person disclosing the problem is the attempt to paraphrase the message just heard. Many peer educators have problems demonstrating
this skill because distractions, both external and internal, can get
in the way and result in missing aspects of the message.

External Distractions

Often distractions in the immediate environment can undercut effective listening. Moving to another location can, in most instances,
quickly alleviate distraction from the hallway, a television or stereo,
or other sources of noise. If this is not possible, you will have to really concentrate to hear effectively.

Internal Distractions

Simply stated, these are thoughts that interfere with listening. Internal distractions are more difficult to alleviate and require greater
levels of personal energy and concentration to overcome. It is necessary to shut down the flow of internal commentary and allow the
entire message of the student to enter your world. This will take
some effort and practice on your part, but it can be done.

Empathic Understanding

This is a critical dimension to interpersonal communication. To be
empathic is to understand the other's world through their frame of

reference and to know how they think and feel in regard to the content of the message they are delivering. Remember, this is how they feel, not how you would feel if caught up in the same type of problem. Empathy is not sympathy. The more effective you are with the skills of attending and listening, the better your ability to empathize with the student you are assisting will become. You will find that the ability to communicate empathy is a powerful helping tool. When you demonstrate this skill, the other person will realize that you are truly listening to their concerns and understanding them and their unique world. In turn, you will aid them in developing better personal understanding.

Interchangeable Responses

In the early stages of a helping relationship, requiring your active use of interpersonal communication skills, you will demonstrate that you are listening intently and understanding the problem you are hearing through a series of responses that are, in effect, interchangeable with the message you have just heard. That is, you will paraphrase what the student has just told you. For example, a student who is experiencing problems with an academic adviser may say, "I can't believe the time I wasted this morning. Dr. Jones and I had an appointment to discuss my spring schedule and I waited an hour and he never showed up. This is the second time he has done this to me." An appropriate interchangeable response in this situation might be, "It seems that you're really annoyed because Dr. Jones failed to show for your advising appointment. Being the second time this has happened makes it even more irritating to you." This response is interchangeable. It captures both the content and feelings being expressed by the student and allows the student the opportunity to continue to self-explore the problem. At the beginning of a helping interaction you will not know where the student may be heading. That is, self-exploration on the part of the student seeking help may lead down many avenues of self-understanding and eventual problem resolution. It is the helper's job to provide the proper conditions (structure) for this process to occur. The interchangeable response will be a powerful helping tool as you aid a student in this process.

Exercise 2: Listening and Responding Skills

1. Find a partner to practice your interchangeable communication skills. First, have your partner say a short sentence (about ten or fifteen words). Now, repeat the sentence word for word. Practice this exercise until you can repeat exactly what your partner said.

2. Once you can repeat a sentence verbatim, turn your attention to practicing paraphrases. Now ask your partner to tell you a story about himself or herself. Paraphrase the story. Can you do this without leaving out any significant details?

3. Ask your partner to share some personal or academic problem. Afterwards, use a word to describe how you think your partner feels as a result of this problem. Ask your partner if you have correctly identified the feeling.

4. Ask your partner to share another personal or academic concern. This time paraphrase back the content you heard and the feeling you think your partner is experiencing. This is an interchangeable response.

Your trainer may spend some time asking you to practice these activities in your training group.

Demonstrating a Nonjudgmental Attitude

You must refrain, within this type of helping relationship, from interjecting your values, opinions, attitudes, and beliefs in regard to the issues being dealt with by the student you are assisting. It is important to take a neutral rather than personally biased stance. Whatever the problem, it must be resolved from within the student's unique world and values—not yours. A solution that works quite well for you may be completely inappropriate or undesirable for the student seeking your help.

There are several factors for you to keep in mind to help you determine if you can remain nonjudgmental within a helping interaction. Three involve your own personal perspective and life situation—your values, the personal life problems you are working on currently, and other unresolved personal or academic problems you have decided not to actively resolve at this time in your life. The fourth deals with the complexity of the problem being presented.

Your Personal Values

From time to time, you may find it impossible to assume this nonjudgmental attitude because of your values and beliefs. For example, consider the pro-life advocate who is trying to assist a young woman trying to resolve an unwanted pregnancy and is considering an abortion. It would be very difficult for a person who advocates pro-life to remain nonjudgmental in this situation. The appropriate course of action for a peer educator in this position is to refer the student to a more neutral person.

Your Current Problems

It is very difficult to assist another person who is having a problem similar to one that you may be experiencing in your own life. For example, a peer educator who is currently struggling through a broken relationship will find it difficult to separate personal feelings and circumstances so as to truly enter, in a nonjudgmental manner, the world of a student seeking assistance in this area. While sympathy will be high with the problem, true empathy will be difficult. Referral to another helper who does not have these personal identification issues is recommended.

Unresolved Personal Concerns

There will be times when students share problems with you that resemble personal and or academic challenges that you have not
achieved or mastered. It is very common for a person to have unresolved concerns and choose not to work on them, despite knowing
that it would be better to do so. Perhaps the level of anxiety generated by the problem is not severe enough to inspire the hard work
necessary to resolve it, but whatever the reason, the person knows
there is work to be done and is avoiding it. Such a person is not
going to be able to sit still and help others do that work for themselves. For example, a peer educator who has not yet chosen a major
and is not actively pursuing a problem-solving approach in deciding the question will, in all likelihood, not be very much assistance
to another undecided student. It would be too easy to enter into
your own frame of reference of also being undecided to give the type
of nonjudgmental helping that is described here. Again, these types
of situations mandate a referral to another helping person.

Complexity of the Problem

Some problems are too complex for peer educators to help others
resolve. Many of these involve personal and interpersonal issues
that, given the age and life history of the student, should have been
mastered long before reaching college. Examples of these *significant
personal concerns* include students who are experiencing problems
that cause them to be severely depressed or perhaps dysfunctional.
These students may be withdrawn, sad, and have little appetite; they
may display antisocial behavior. There are reasons for these types of
behaviors with associated problems that must be solved. A peer educator is not the best person to work with these concerns, and a referral to a more qualified helper is required in these situations. Any
time you hear problems from other students that indicate to you that
they may be a threat to themselves (suicidal thoughts or plans) or
others in the community (threatening others), you are involved in

a helping relationship that goes beyond most peer educators' expertise. Also, if you feel nervous and upset when listening to another student's problem, you are in a problem area that is over your head from a helping perspective. Refer these students to your supervisor or another more experienced helper.

Reflection Point 3

Think of a time in the past when you have assisted a friend with a problem that was causing anxiety or distress:

What approach did you take when you helped this person (did you just listen, give advice, help discuss options)?

_____

_____

_____

So what approach would you now take if confronted with the same situation?

_____

_____

_____

Now what can you do to begin to acquire the skills necessary to implement this approach?

_____

_____

_____

Implementing the Model

Besides using your interpersonal communication skills when you begin a helping relationship, you will most often have to use these skills to demonstrate your concern and interest with students who are experiencing some degree of distress but can not pinpoint its origin.

Students in distress need to self-explore to understand the nature of their concern. Once they understand, they can employ more active problem-solving strategies.

To implement effective interpersonal communications by employing the skills we have described, it is necessary that you recognize that this communication is divided into two parts. You must both send messages effectively and receive messages effectively. The following material—from Ender, Saunders-McCaffrey, and Miller, 1979, pp. 57–59—describes the process of sending and receiving messages.

Sending Messages

Sending a message may seem instinctive—after all, you have been talking for as long as you can remember. Nonetheless, there are several principles that will make your communications much more effective than they are likely to be if you just say the first thing that comes to mind.

Own Your Messages by Saying "I" and "My"

Personal ownership includes clearly taking responsibility for the ideas and feelings that you express. Individuals disown their messages when they use terms like *most people, everybody,* or *all of us.* Such terms, when you use them in your role as a peer educator, make it difficult for the person you are trying to assist to tell whether you really think and feel what you are saying or whether the statement represents the thoughts and feelings of others.

Make Your Messages Complete and Specific

Include clear statements of all necessary information the receiver needs in order to comprehend the message. Being complete and specific seems obvious, but often an individual you are helping will not understand your frame of reference, the assumptions you have made, the intentions for your communication, or the leaps in thinking you have taken. While the person may hear the words, comprehension of the meaning of the message may be lost if you fail to be both specific and complete with your thoughts.

Make Your Verbal and Nonverbal Messages Congruent

When using interpersonal communication skills, both verbal and nonverbal messages will be communicated. In most cases, these messages should be congruent. For example, a person who is expressing genuine appreciation of someone's help will usually be smiling and expressing warmth in nonverbal ways. Communication problems can occur when a person's verbal and nonverbal messages are contradictory. For instance, think how you'd react if a person were to say, "Here is some information that I thought you could use," but with a sneering face and a mocking tone of voice. The impression received is confused by the two different messages being sent simultaneously.

Use Redundancy

Repeat your messages more than once, using more than one channel of communication to do so. This will help the receiver understand your messages.

Ask for Feedback

To communicate effectively you must be aware of how the receiver is interpreting and processing your messages. The only way to be sure is to continually seek feedback concerning what meanings the receiver is attaching to your messages.

Make the Message Appropriate to the Receiver's Frame of Reference

The same information may need different explanations depending on whether you're talking to an expert in the field or to a novice, to a child or to an adult, to your boss or to a coworker. You must work hard to ensure that you do not over- or underestimate the capacity of the receiver to understand what you have to say.

Describe Your Feelings by Name, Action, or Figures of Speech

Within this framework of helping, you will be working hard to assist the other person to discover how they feel regarding the situation you are exploring. It is extremely important, therefore, that you are also descriptive in the explanation of your own feelings. You may describe your feelings by name ("feel proud of your accomplishment"), or actions ("Your accomplishment makes me feel like dancing on a cloud"). Use of these types of descriptions will help to communicate your feelings clearly and unambiguously. Also, by describing your feelings you, in turn, are modeling the way to aptly identify and express this important dimension of communication.

Describe Behavior Without Evaluating or Interpreting

When responding to the behavior of other people, make sure to describe their behavior rather than evaluating it. For example, "your talking while I speak makes me lose my train of thought" rather than "you are being rude."

Receiving Messages

When using interpersonal communication skills, you must not only send messages effectively, you must also receive messages effectively. Skills in this area include the following:

Listening

Being an effective listener means that you are capable of recognizing both the content of the message being sent and the speaker's feelings and needs.

Paraphrasing

You must be able to hear the message so clearly that you can paraphrase back to the speaker, in a nonevaluative way, both the content of the message and the feelings the speaker is experiencing in regard to that content. For example, say a student asks for your time to share a problem but then beats around the bush and seems uncomfortable being specific about the nature of their concern. You might respond, "You indicate that you have a personal concern, but you don't seem to feel free to share it with me."

Communicating Empathy

You must be able to describe what you perceive to be the sender's feelings. For example, you might say, "You seem to be quite anxious about your visit with your parents."

Interpreting

Applying all of the aforementioned skills in receiving messages, you must, as accurately as possible, communicate your understanding of both the content and feelings you have heard. Rather than defending your initial understanding, you must then negotiate with the sender until there is agreement as to the sender's message.

Applying Interpersonal Communication Skills

When applying these types of communication skills in a helping relationship, the goal is not to solve the problems of others but to help them explore ways to better understand their own problems, develop and evaluate alternatives, set some personal courses of action, and then carry it out. Many people who have had help in the self-exploration and understanding phase can create alternatives and begin to take action on their own. What is most needed is a non-judgmental, objective person to help them examine the personal dissonance they were experiencing. Once the source of this dissonance is brought into the light, many can go on to active problem solving. On the other hand, for some people, understanding the problem is only the first phase of the helping relationship. They will need the peer educator to continue to provide assistance in identifying alternatives, evaluating these alternatives, and charting a course of action. This section—taken from Ender, Saunders-McCaffrey, and Miller, 1979, pp. 59–60—will focus only on the self-exploration and self-understanding phase of the helping relationship. The next chapter will present many strategies a peer educator can implement when assisting another with the development of alternatives and action phases of problem resolution.

Self-Exploration Leads to Self-Understanding

Even though it seems obvious, you must constantly remember that you cannot help anyone, nor can they help themselves, if you and they do not understand the problem. If you do not know where a person is at the moment, you cannot help them get somewhere else. Also, keep in mind that what people frequently share with you initially is not necessarily what is really bothering them. Most people seeking help with personal problems will want to assure themselves that the person helping is trustworthy and competent as a helper. They are checking the water, so to speak, prior to jumping in. You must earn the right and privilege of helping another. This will occur during the early phase of the helping relationship if you are demonstrating the skills of effective interpersonal communication. Suffice to say, make sure both you and the person you are helping agree that the real problem that is bothering them has been identified prior to moving on to problem-solving and action phases. How do you do this? Here are some ideas.

Acknowledge Feelings

Acknowledge the person's feelings and inferences. If the other person sounds depressed, you acknowledge this feeling by saying, "You sound pretty depressed [up-tight, unhappy, sad, whatever]." If the person sounds angry, frustrated, or disappointed, acknowledge that. This indicates that you are listening and, more important, understanding the person. If the student sounds unhappy with you personally, acknowledge this also: "It sounds like you don't feel that I am being too helpful" or "You sound angry [disappointed, frustrated, whatever] with me."

Make It Clear

You need to clarify or ask for clarification of any idea, or any word, that you feel that you do not understand. Take nothing for granted. You may find the following phrases helpful in clarifying things: "I'm not sure I understand what you mean by [whatever]," or "It is not clear to me exactly what your situation is." "Could you tell me more about that?" "Can you give me an example of [whatever it is]?" These are phrases that may work for you, but may not sound right if you parrot them. Use phrases that are your own, phrases with which you are comfortable.

Check Your Understanding

One of the best ways to check your understanding of what someone is saying is to repeat it back to them in slightly different terms. You can lead into this by saying, "If I understand you, what you are saying is [paraphrase]." Or "Let's see if I understand; what I hear you saying is [paraphrase]."

In this self-exploration and understanding phase, you are, in effect, a sounding board for the person you are trying to help. You are mirroring their thoughts and feelings, attempting to help them determine the source of their dissonance.

Keep in mind that students will present a range of problems as they deal with the various challenges of college life. As noted in Chapter Two, these include challenges in the areas of intellectual and academic adjustment, physical well-being, academic concerns, significant personal and academic concerns, and problems in interpersonal relationships, career and lifestyle choices, and the unique demands faced by adult students.

Summary

The types of interpersonal communication skills described in this chapter are quite different from those used in day-to-day conversations with others. In the context of a helping relationship, effective interpersonal communication skills are complex and require substantial practice to implement successfully. Primarily, within this relationship, you are expressing your ability to listen effectively and with empathy. You express these skills through the responses you give as the student self-explores the problem and gains deeper levels of self-understanding. During the initial stage of this type of relationship, it is best to stick to facilitating self-help and to avoid assuming an intrusive helping approach. In the next chapter you will explore several types of problem-solving strategies you may choose to initiate with a student after the problem has been fully explored, clarified, and understood.

———————

Chapter Four: Summary Questions

1. In your own words, describe the major differences between normal day-to-day interactions and the special qualities of employing effective interpersonal communication skills in a helping relationship.

———————————————————————————
———————————————————————————
———————————————————————————
———————————————————————————
———————————————————————————

2. Give five reasons why advice giving is an inappropriate response in a helping relationship.

———————————————————————————
———————————————————————————
———————————————————————————
———————————————————————————
———————————————————————————

3. Define empathy.

———————————————————————————
———————————————————————————

4. What is an interchangeable response?

———————————————————————————
———————————————————————————

5. Describe situations where it is best to turn to another helping person.

———————————————————————————
———————————————————————————
———————————————————————————

———————

5

Problem Solving with Individuals

Learning Objectives

After completing this chapter the peer educators will be able to

1. Demonstrate effective interpersonal communication skills while assisting students in problem-solving activities.

2. Identify the source of problem situations by applying assessment methods that promote exploration and analysis of a problem area.

3. Describe interview techniques and assessment tools designed to assist in the assessment process.

4. Explain the characteristic properties of successful goal statements.

5. Describe the relationship of behavioral objectives to goal setting and problem solving.

6. Formulate action plans that include processes for monitoring progress and attainment of goals.

7. Apply alternative, creative problem-solving strategies.

———————

Chapter Four introduced the concept of interpersonal communication skills and their uses in working with students who are seeking a peer educator's understanding and personal involvement as they work to identify and solve problems. These skills, when practiced effectively, can produce quite positive results as an individual works through the self-exploration and understanding phases of problem solving. However, identifying a problem and actually solving that problem are two different issues. This chapter will focus on the problem-solving or action phase of problem resolution.

College students face an array of problems that can include deciding what courses to take, figuring out how to live with a roommate, organizing time and resources, dealing with strong emotions, finding a job, or managing a crisis event. One way to view and organize types of problems is to look at the source of the difficulty the person is having.

De Bono (1971 [1967]) describes three conditions that are the source of problems. The first is where a person is experiencing a *gap*. A gap is a deficit, which could be a lack of information, an absence of knowledge, or a deficiency in skill. A second condition is described as a *barrier*. A barrier is an obstacle that is getting in the way of accomplishing a desired direction or goal. A barrier may be created by perceived personal limits, such as lack of confidence, indecision, or confusion. A barrier may also be outside the individual, caused by factors in the environment, lack of resources, or restrictions on behavior created by a social order such as the school, the church, the government, or the family. The third type of problems come from dealing with an *unknown*, or novel situation. When venturing into uncharted areas, a person lacks past experience and is uncertain what is needed to prepare for the future. The novel situation demands that a person explore new possibilities and be able to find creative solutions. Identifying the source and type of problem is a helpful prerequisite for determining the avenue to a solution.

An effective problem-solving approach starts with defining the problem from a positive perspective. In other words, the opposite side of the coin when experiencing a gap, barrier, or unknown situation is the *desirable outcome*. It is a description of what and where the person would like to be when the problem is resolved. The positive outcome is the hoped-for goal. Understanding why a person is unable to reach the desired goal requires an *assessment* of the problem. An assessment is the process of gathering important information that analyzes both the negative sources of concern about the problem and the positive resources for solution. Once an analysis of the factors surrounding a problem is made, it is possible to devise a plan of action that includes the steps and strategies necessary to reach a goal, along with methods to monitor progress and goal achievement.

As a peer educator, you are likely to find it tempting to concentrate on specific problem-solving strategies such as the ones presented in this chapter. However, it is again important to note that a prerequisite for becoming a facilitator of problem solution is the use of effective interpersonal communication skills described in Chapter Four. Your accurate listening and clear responses provide a sounding board for students who are exploring problems, promoting self-understanding and insights leading to problem resolution. Clarification and understanding of a problem area will then lead to a more action-oriented stage of problem solving.

Strategies for Problem Resolution

Resolving problems will require work and energy on your part and from the student who has sought your assistance. The next section (adapted in part from Ender, Saunders-McCaffrey, and Miller, 1979) will discuss specific principles and methods for implementing goal setting, assessment, behavioral objectives, action plans, and outcome monitors.

Goal Setting

As the old saying goes, "If you do not know where you are going, you will never know if you have arrived!" It is critically important that students attempting to resolve problems have a clear understanding of what they are trying to accomplish. The vision of a desired outcome must be determined prior to entering the assessment and behavioral objective phases of problem resolution. There are several characteristics typical to goal setting that provide the best opportunity for successful problem resolution. These characteristics include personal relevance, positiveness, clarity, and a reasonable level of attainability.

Successful Goals Are Relevant to the Person

Many individuals have established goals that are not really their own—that is, these goals are more important to someone else in the student's life than to the student theoretically pursuing them. For example, many students choose academic majors that may have resulted more from the encouragement and desires of parents, teachers, or friends than from their own initiative. Unfortunately, a major chosen in this way may have little in common with the student's values, interests, and abilities. It is usual for a person to find it difficult to meet the challenge of hard work and energy required to accomplish something when the effort lacks personal meaning and value. The following exercise challenges you to place yourself at the center of choosing significant life goals.

Exercise 1: The Board of Directors

Consider an important life decision that may be confronting you during the next several months. Many examples come to mind—changing a major, deciding on where to live, transferring to another college, purchasing a car. Whatever the issue, to determine your preferences in making this decision, pretend that you will call together a Board of Directors. This Board of Directors provides input into the decisions you make even though you will eventually cast the deciding vote. On this board, you may place several significant people in your life from whom you value input. For example, you might include on the board your best friend, your parents, an adviser, someone you consider an expert, and an admired teacher. However, an important rule to establish the priority of personal input is that you must appoint yourself to chair the board and maintain at least a 51 percent interest in the voting power of all decisions. On the first line, under the heading "Problem Description" (below) describe the problem to be solved or decision to be made. On the next few lines name the other members of your board, and place the options or inputs that you and the members of your board might suggest. Let's say that the decision to be made involves the purchase of a car. The inputs from board members suggest that you should consider factors such as gas mileage, dependability, needs for the future, and budget considerations. A hypothetical discussion determines which of the above factors are most important and three different choices are offered by your board (getting a loan and buying a newer model car, getting an older car with a reputation for good service, assuming payments on a relative's car who is looking for a new car). Place a percentage of voting input for each person and take a vote on the options (remember you have 51 percent!).

Problem Description:

_____

Board Members:

_____

_____

_____

Options:

_____

_____

_____

_____

Vote:

_____

_____

_____

Goals Should Be Stated Positively

Positive thinking will improve the chances for successful goal attainment. Even when starting with a problem situation, it is best to understand that the flip side of a negative concern is a positive goal. For instance, if you did poorly on an exam and are concerned about getting a low grade in a class, it is best to describe your goal in positive terms. Rather than saying, "What do I need to do to avoid getting a 'D' or failing this class?" it is better to say "What are the steps I can take to be successful and get a 'B' in this class?" Positive thinking usually generates energy and excitement, while negative thinking typically produces feelings of drudgery and boredom. In your role, assist others by promoting positive thinking and outcomes.

Exercise 2: Negatives to Positives

On the following spaces, list three problem situations you are facing and then restate those situations as positive goals.

The Problem: The Positive Goal:

1. _____   1. _____

   _____   _____

2. _____   2. _____

   _____   _____

Goals Must Be Clear and Explicit

It is quite helpful in the goal-setting process to encourage others to write down their goals as specifically as possible. Writing can help clarify and crystallize the thought process. It also helps provide ownership for the student, because, once written, the goal becomes concrete and real. To assist the student to write a precise goal with specific outcomes, you can use the goal attainment process that will be discussed later in the chapter.

Goals Must Be Attainable with a Stretch

For goals to feel worth pursuing, they must be realistic and attainable. At the same time, it is important that a person stretch and extend if they desire to use their full potential. For instance, for a student who desires to obtain a level of personal fitness but does not like to run, a goal of entering and completing a marathon a couple of months after beginning a fitness program would provide very little inspiration or motivation. On the other hand, someone who does like to run and has finished long-distance races in the past probably could reach this goal after developing and completing a proper training program—and is therefore much more likely to find it worth trying. A well-stated goal would make a person reach beyond the present position, but should not be out of sight. It is useful to describe a goal with specific details from four levels—backsliding, current performance, easy improvement, and serious stretch. For example, if the goal of a student was to increase the quantity of study time so as to increase preparedness for class, these four perspectives could be written as follows:

Level 1: A description of behavior if you were to fall back or do worse.

Example: I would study an average of less than two hours per day.

Level 2: An accurate description of the present behavior.

Example: I now study an average of two hours each day during the week, and three hours on weekend days.

Level 3: A description of behavior that is an improvement within easy reach.

Example: I would study an additional half hour a day, and an extra hour on weekends.

Level 4: A description of behavior that would stretch beyond your immediate reach.

Example: I would double my study time each day and include an extra three hours on weekends.

Exercise 3: Goal Attainment Scaling

Identify one immediate goal you have in your life at the present time. Choose a very specific area, such as increase your exercise, meet and make new friends, improve note-taking skills, or reduce time watching television. Remember, if using a problem such as watching television, change the negative into a positive goal by stating it in a manner such as, "I desire to increase the productivity of my free time." After stating the goal, describe your present level, then note a level below (backsliding), and two improved levels (immediate reach and extended reach).

Goal: _____

Level 1 (below present level): _____

Level 2 (present level): _____

Level 3 (immediate reach): _____

Level 4 (beyond immediate reach): _____

Setting goals allows a person to take control of life. Goals provide direction and meaning to each day. Goals promote an individual's sense of self-direction and accountability, and also allow the individual to determine if the behaviors being exhibited on a day-to-day basis are congruent with the desired destination.

Reflection Point 1

Think about goal statements:

What are the qualities of goal statements that afford an optimal chance for success? Restate these qualities in your own words. Now imagine a situation in which you had a goal that did not meet these four qualities.

_____

_____

So what is apt to result if the goal is not relevant, positive, clear, and attainable. Can you give examples of
such a goal that you have held and describe the result?

_____

_____

_____

_____

Now what strategies could you use when setting future
goals to best assure your success?

_____

_____

_____

_____

_____

Assessment

Assessment is a process that assists in locating the source of a problem. Does the person have a gap, such as a lack of information, skill
deficiency, or missing resource? Is the person facing a barrier from
within, such as a lack of confidence or personal confusion? Or is the
barrier a conflict with others or with sources in the environment?
The assessment process helps pinpoint the origin of the problem
concern, which can then lead to determining what needs to be done
to attain that goal. Assessment will further assist in charting the
course and making a plan to be followed.

If practiced successfully, assessment is the starting point for goal
accomplishment. For students seeking to declare an academic major,
there are several types of information about each student that should
be assessed. For instance, do they have a clear idea of their own interests, skills, or capabilities? Are they knowledgeable about the various majors offered on campus? Do they know what careers may

result from a major? Do they know about job opportunities, requirements, and world of work prospects? If not, do they know the resources available for them to gain this information? The structured
informational interview is designed to ask these types of questions
and begin the assessment process.

Structured Interview Techniques

The assessment interview is the most common way to get information by following a deliberate format to gather information about
someone's concerns, locate the sources of problems, and assess
strengths and weaknesses. The assessment interview operates from
the basic principles of the interpersonal communication model discussed in the preceding chapter. Peer educators must follow a process in which active listening, respectful communication, and
empathy become the cornerstones of the helping interaction. The
following steps are examples of how the interview can be structured.

1. Ask open-ended questions that allow students you are helping
   to express their situation from their own perspective and in
   their own words. Take the example of a student who wants to
   improve physical fitness. Asking someone to describe what it
   would be like to be fit—permitting the student to elaborate
   on their own thoughts—is better than asking a yes-or-no
   question such as "Do you do aerobics?"

2. Follow up leads of information from what a student provides
   from the open-ended questions by asking for clarification and
   expansion of specific points. "Tell me more about—" or "Help
   me to understand—" will seek further elaboration of what has
   been said.

3. Use paraphrasing and summaries of the student's responses
   to help pinpoint what the student sees as the source of the
   problem.

4. After gathering background information, make a tentative
   hypothesis of what the student has described about the prob-

lem. Examples that represent some of the diagnostic alternatives follow:

Gaps: Lack knowledge about self

Lack information about options in the world around them

Lack skills

Barriers: Confusion or conflict within self

Conflict with others

Limits within self, such as lack of confidence

Limits from environment, such as lack of support

Unknowns: Inexperienced in area

Tunnel vision with old solutions; need new possibilities

Now state the tentative hypothesis so the student can verify the diagnosis or determine the need to question the hypothesis and explore the problem further.

5. Reframe the problem into a positive goal statement.

6. Identify where there is potential need for further informal or formal assessment tools. The following section describes the ways that other forms of assessments can be obtained on a college campus.

Informal techniques for making an assessment may include checklists, surveys, or self-report questionnaires that are locally developed by your organization or sponsoring agency. They might also include surveys obtained from sources of authoritative information, such as library resources or even reliable Internet sites. These tools may measure a wide range of student needs and interest in categories that include study habits, eating behaviors, wellness, career preferences, assertiveness, dating behaviors, stress reactions, and many more.

Formal assessment tools are more standardized tests and measuring instruments that are frequently available through professional offices on campus. For example, a student making choices about academic majors and career directions may need to have measures of personal interests, values, likes, and dislikes to various academic majors, career fields, and occupations. Interactive computer programs that explore career choice are available on most campuses—titles include *Discover*, produced by American College Testing, or *SIGI PLUS*, produced by the Educational Testing Service. Also, a career center or counseling service will offer career assessments such as the *Campbell Interest and Skills Inventory* or the *Strong Interest Inventory*. Academic study habits may be assessed with instruments such as the *Survey of Study Habits and Attitudes*. In most cases your role as a peer educator will be to help direct students to offices in which the formal assessments are conducted, such as career centers, counseling centers, wellness centers, health education offices, recreation centers, or academic assistance centers. In some cases, you may be working with an office in which you will be trained and prepared to assist students with computer interactive assessments and survey instruments.

Self-Report Techniques

Many students can benefit from analyzing their present behavior (establishing a baseline of data) prior to determining a plan of action for change. For example, students who desire to practice better time management would benefit from monitoring their present time management practices for several days. They could keep a daily log to determine how they are using their time. An examination of this log, with the assistance of the peer educator, will lead to the discovery of how time is wasted. Using this baseline data, a better schedule can be determined and experimented with. This same technique can be used when establishing better nutrition or exercise programs. It is always helpful to have a clear understanding of present behavior prior to attempting to change to behavior that is deemed more successful or positive.

Behavioral Observation

Another excellent method to assist students as they gather information about themselves is behavioral observation and feedback. For instance, students learning effective job interviewing techniques can be videotaped as they participate in mock interviews. Students can then observe themselves on tape and areas of interviewing strengths and weaknesses can be highlighted, leading to practice in any weak areas. This same technique is also helpful as students learn group leadership skills, the interpersonal communication skills model introduced in the preceding chapter, or any other skill that requires an assortment of behavioral skill development.

Force-Field Analysis:
Systematic Assessment of Strengths and Weaknesses

Lewin (1951) originally developed Force-Field Analysis and over the years it has become a commonly used method to map a plan for goal attainment. *Driving* and *restraining* forces describe factors that inhibit or enhance one's progress toward a goal. Drivers are actions that should produce positive results or help lead to positive outcomes. Restrainers are actions that seem to take away from intended outcomes. The identification of these forces can then lead to a plan of action. The student solving a problem identifies both types of forces and brainstorms activities that would help to eliminate the restraining forces and implement the driving forces. Choices are then made to select the activities that would provide the best chances for success to implement a reasonable plan of action. The following exercise illustrates this process.

Exercise 4: Force-Field Analysis

This exercise starts from the point where you have identified a problem and then restated that problem into a positive goal statement. The next step is to recognize the forces that will push toward improvement and attainment of the goal (driving forces) and those forces that will re-sist improvement (restraining forces) and maintain the sit-uation as a problem. For example, if a goal was to improve overall physical fitness, driving forces might include reg-ular cardiovascular exercise, good nutrition, and regular sleep. Factors that could deter the attainment of fitness could include eating too many sweets, watching television while lying on the couch, or drinking too much alcohol.

Step 1: Write one of your goal statements from Exer-cise 2 on the line labeled for the purpose below.

Driving Forces: (1)   (2)   (3)   (4)

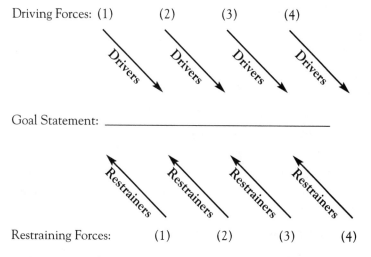

Goal Statement: _____

Restraining Forces: (1)   (2)   (3)   (4)

Step 2: On the sets of lines above and below the goal statement, describe at least four driving and four re-straining forces that would affect attainment of the de-sired outcome.

Step 3: For each restraining force, list possible action steps that you could plan and carry out to reduce the ef-fect of that force or eliminate it completely. For example, if your goal is to be able to study early in the morning and a restraining force is your tendency to sleep through the alarm, you might get a louder alarm, go to bed earlier, or have someone personally wake you up.

_____

_____

_____

_____

Step 4: Similarly, think of as many possibilities as you can for implementing each of the driving forces. After completing a list of possible ways to enhance driving forces and reduce restraining forces, prioritize these potential problem-solving activities in order to target the most likely activities for success.

_____

_____

_____

_____

_____

The Action Plan: Objectives and Activities

Once you and the student you are working with know what you are trying to accomplish (goal) and the student's strengths and weaknesses (determined through assessment) in regard to readiness, you have a starting point for goal completion. It is now necessary to determine a specific plan of action. This is accomplished through the development of specific objectives that describe the student's intentions in an observable and measurable manner. Behavioral objectives spell out and make the plan recognizable in tangible ways. Objectives might include activities such as interviewing people, reading information, writing a letter, and demonstrating or practicing a skill. The key is the notion of observability. Behavioral objectives are designed to move the student to goal accomplishment. The information gathered in the assessment stage of problem resolution determines the specific behaviors that need to be implemented to achieve the desired goal or outcome. In effect, this stage is similar to developing a contract or agreement—a blueprint that the student can use to chart progress and measure the eventual outcome.

The action plan for problem resolution is a list of behavioral objectives which, once completed, should lead to goal accomplishment. The peer educator assists in the formulation of these behavioral objectives and seeks to help the student determine that nothing has been left out. As the plan is being implemented the peer educator may wish to create checkpoints—scheduled meetings to assess specific accomplishments that will provide a measure of how well the plan is going and how successfully the student is progressing toward goal completion. During these sessions, the plan may need to be changed or amended if new information and progress assessment suggest adjustments that will improve the chances for success.

It is obvious that action plans are never set in concrete, as, by definition, they are plans in action. Refinement is often necessary and follow up with students is essential for optimizing on success. Completion of goals often leads to new areas of exploration and action plans. Life is always a work in process!

Outcome Evaluations

The final stage of resolving a problem and achieving a goal is knowing that you have reached completion. Peer educators can assist students in this process through the use of formative and summative evaluation techniques.

Formative Evaluation

Formative evaluation is the process of analyzing the progress of goal completion as it is occurring. As students move toward goal accomplishment, it is often necessary to review the process periodically. This requires follow-up interviews between the peer helper and the student. These interviews are designed to make sure the student is staying on track. It is helpful to review the plan of action and determine if anything has been left out. Data gathered while progressing toward goal completion should be discussed. New or expanded strategies should be formulated if necessary.

Summative Evaluation

Summative evaluation is the process of determining if the goal has been accomplished and success achieved. Did the goal, once met, have the desired effect? For example, is the student satisfied with the outcome or has the accomplishment of this goal led to other questions or concerns? Again, in the area of academic majors, the student may have accomplished the goal of declaring a major. However, in the process of completing this goal, new questions regarding internships, minors, or other aspects of academic study may have arisen. The summative assessment process often leads to the development of new goals and behavioral objectives.

Creative Strategies to Explore New Places

The preceding problem-solving activity presents one coherent system when assisting another person in problem solving. The process of problem identification, goal setting, assessment of strengths and weaknesses, development of behavioral objectives, and constant refinement through assessment interviews can be helpful when addressing many types of student concerns. However, it doesn't always work. People may find themselves in territory where they have little if any previous experience. They also may experience a nearly opposite yet equally trying situation in which they face a problem that seems very familiar but the old and commonplace ways of acting in that situation are not producing results. In these cases, the use of assessment, analysis, and objective options may not be sufficient to resolve the problem. An option to explore the unknown or to break the tunnel vision of commonplace solutions is to use *creative problem-solving* methods.

Creative problem solving uses the principles of fluency, suspension of judgment, free association, mental stimulation, and artistic expression (Prince, 1971). *Fluency* describes a process of seeking a quantity of solution alternatives without regard for outcome. Generating alternatives is best done in an atmosphere of *suspended judgment,* in which analysis is set aside so that one does not thwart or inhibit possibilities. The process of *free association* happens when people feel free to follow any tangent or whim that comes to mind, building quickly from a word, an image, or an idea. *Mental stimulation* describes the process of unlocking the mind to look at old patterns in new and different ways. *Artistic expression* requires one to use the mechanisms of the intuitive holistic process and tie various elements together into one image, the artistic product, which might be as elaborate as a poem, song, picture, or the like, or as simple and spontaneous as a metaphor dropped into a conversation.

Roger von Oech (1986) recommends four roles for implementing the creative problem-solving process. You are an *explorer* when you search for new information and options. You become an *artist* when turning possibilities and resources into new ideas. In the third stage you become a *judge* to assimilate and evaluate the merits of an idea. In the final stage, you become a *warrior* to boldly and courageously implement a new idea. The strategies below will introduce peer educators to some simple strategies to generate creative possibilities in problem solving.

Reflection Point 2

Think about personal attitudes and mind-sets:

What do you believe would be most helpful for enhancing the opportunity to think in new and creative ways?

_____

_____

_____

So what atmosphere, setting, or artistic medium would promote your exploration?

_____

_____

_____

Now what ways would you use to generate a far-out idea in your quest for solving a problem or finding a new opportunity?

_____

_____

_____

_____

Brainstorming is a helpful technique to operate with a divergent thinking model to explore and consider many new and even far-out possibilities. When one brainstorms, judgment of the worthiness of ideas generated is withheld for later scrutiny—brainstorming, by definition, is the generation of options without evaluation of the merits of those options. It allows for free thinking, spontaneity, creativity, and the free association of ideas.

Perhaps, as a peer educator, you are working with a student who is bothered by a troublesome roommate. The student would like to live in more harmony with the roommate and is troubled by the roommate's lack of consideration. This person is quite messy and leaves clothes, books, papers, food, and an assortment of personal items scattered throughout the room. The student you are helping is unsure of what plan of action to implement and you suggest brainstorming some alternatives for consideration. These could include ideas like ignoring the situation, confronting the roommate with the bothersome behavior, talking to the residence hall staff, picking up after the roommate, modeling more appropriate behavior, drawing a line on the floor and telling the roommate to never cross it, moving out, or spending a lot of time with a friend and storing critical belongings in their room. Pushing the freewheeling even further provides even wilder ideas like hiring the "cat-in-the-hat," designing a wall separator, or creating a loft to seal off two separate areas. Some—perhaps most—of these ideas are pretty silly, but the key to this process is generating as many options as possible for consideration. After the options are on the table, it is important to enter the artist phase.

Metaphors and Other Artistic Designs

During the artist phase, the task is to incorporate the creative ideas together into a picture that pulls various elements of a problem situation together. A common, everyday strategy for painting a verbal picture is to use metaphors to capture a unique situation that words, using literal definitions, cannot portray. Metaphors provide a screen in which there is openness to possibilities, a flexibility to shift perspectives, and a tolerance for trying out a new or different reality (Newton and Wilson, 1991).

Metaphors can be analogies that compare one's situation to another circumstance. For example, a student may share frustration with mastering a course assignment by saying, "It is like playing solitaire when the deck has a missing card; no matter how many times I try, I can never win." Solution possibilities may first be looked at within the framework of the metaphor. In response, you might ask, "Are there ways for you to make new rules for the game? Are there games you could play that don't need that card?" The metaphor may provide some distance from the familiar pattern and yet also allow exploration of various options that are in some ways parallel.

Metaphors can be paradoxes, which contrast opposing extremes in ways that help make new connections. Two roommates describe a conflict in which one likes the room hot while the other likes to sleep cool. Their problem might be addressed as experiencing what it would be like to "store ice cream in an oven" or "enjoy the benefits of a warm summer day while living at the North Pole." To experience the different perspectives through metaphor, one can "become," or personalize acting "as if" they are the metaphor, and then look for solutions after experiencing the contrast and looking for mutual benefits.

A third way to use metaphor is to experience the problem as a story or fantasy. This is illustrated by the science fiction television show *Star Trek: The Next Generation*. The starship has a special chamber called the Holodeck. In this place a computer simulator can create a whole new environment and the person entering can escape into a fantasy to explore, rearrange, or try out new, imaginable possibilities. Providing students the opportunity to create and arrange their ideal fantasy of what they had previously experienced as a difficult problem can aid and encourage them in finding new solutions.

Exercise 5: Problems as Metaphors

Identify a problem situation in which you have felt stuck in regard to finding a satisfactory solution. Take a relaxed position in a comfortable chair, close your eyes, and imagine you are able to enter the Holodeck, where you can have a fantasy in which the ideal can come true. Once the ideas begin to form, sit up and write your fantasy as a story with any dream elements that come to mind and suggest to you possibilities without the restrictions of present limits, real or perceived. An alternative exercise would be to think of possible metaphors for any dilemma you face and then to write a story about the metaphor and how you experience being a part of that metaphor.

Judging the Creation

The divergent or expanded thinking that occurs during creativity reaches a point when possible ideas need to be applied back to the problem situation. This is when the problem-solver becomes a judge and makes decisions about which ideas and possibilities seem most worthy for future consideration. Determine the criteria that will be used to make decisions regarding the worthiness of the options remaining. For instance, returning to the roommate conflict situation, here are some criteria that may prove useful: How bothersome is this behavior? How much time is left in the semester? Has the issue been discussed before? and, How comfortable is the student in confronting irritating behavior? Determine which criteria will best guide decision making. Typically there are the seeds of good ideas embedded in many of the options that were brainstormed during the creative phase. The important thing during the judging and analysis phase is to make a "force fit" for finding ways to implement the possibilities into a practical solution. At this point, you may again return to the concrete problem-solving model discussed earlier in this chapter and go through the steps of setting behavioral objectives and process monitoring devices.

Implementing Bold Change

One of the realities of making significant changes from habituated and commonly accepted practice is the challenge and courage needed to implement new options. The person will often feel anxious about trying out new behaviors because they may seem unproven and may have unpredictable results. For this reason, it is important to prepare a person to assume an attitude that they are on an adventure where there are possibilities to make great new discoveries, but also there will be dead ends and setbacks. However, by holding the perspective that even mistakes and dead ends provide important learning, the person can continue to stay open to the new possibilities.

Another barrier for assuming a new behavior or attitude is the initial resistance that may be received from others in one's life— people may become uncomfortable when someone does not act in the predictable way. The person who is trying to change may encounter questions and objections about the new way of acting. Informing friends and family about the choice of a new course and asking for their support is one way to include others from the beginning. However, persistence and determination are qualities that aid all people as they enact change.

Finally, the attainment of any goal in which an investment of time and energy has been committed calls for a celebration of recognition. Ceremonies, rewards, and the sharing of recognition with important people in one's life should be built into any action plan.

Summary

This chapter has introduced and given examples of several strategies that can be used when assisting others with problem situations. The strategies of goal setting, assessment, behavioral objectives, action planning, and creative problem solving have been explored. An understanding of these techniques and their application to specific situations will provide a method for helping students resolve problems.

Chapter Five: Summary Questions

1. List four characteristics of a goal statement.

_____

_____

_____

2. Define:

a. Assessment _____

b. Force-field analysis _____

c. Structured assessment interview _____

d. Self-report techniques _____

e. Behavioral observation _____

f. Formative evaluation _____

g. Summative evaluation _____

h. Creative problem solving _____

i. Brainstorming _____

3. What is the primary characteristic of a behavioral objective?

_____

_____

_____

4. How is formative evaluation used in the action phase of the problem-solving model?

_____

_____

_____

5. How can a force-field analysis be used in conjunction with a brainstorming activity?

_____

_____

_____

_____

Understanding Group Process

Learning Objectives

After completing this chapter the peer educators will be able to

1. Identify the benefits and advantages of the group environment for helping students.

2. Identify positive communication methods in group settings.

3. Understand how group norms are formed.

4. Realize the effects of individual role behavior on group interaction.

5. Identify levels of commitment by members of a group.

6. Understand how the group's task structure can affect decision making and successful accomplishment of goals.

7. Determine how the group's stage of development can affect the needs, behaviors, and productivity of the group.

———————

Groups are everywhere. You were born to a family and taught in class after class, you play on teams, interact with coworkers, live with roommates, and literally experience life as a series of group interactions. While life experience seems to qualify everyone as an expert on how to interact and get along with groups of people, few people look carefully and systematically at this awareness. What makes a group work? Why do you enjoy interacting in certain situations while feeling bored and uninterested in others? When is a group most productive or least productive? How does a group change and evolve over time?

This chapter will provide a focused way to observe your own experience in groups and determine which factors affect a group for better or worse. Concentrating on what is happening within a group and how the group functions is a matter of studying the *process* or *dynamics* of groups. As a peer educator, you will find that the information and activity presented in this chapter increases your awareness of group process and helps you make use of this awareness to increase your effectiveness when working with a group and its member interactions.

Reflection Point 1

Think of a group in which you have taken part and have had a very positive association. Perhaps you experienced the group as enjoyable, fun, productive, engaging, stimulating, or successful. Reflect back on your experience:

What distinguished the group as positive for you?

_____

_____

_____

So what qualities, characteristics, behaviors, or other such processes contributed to the success of the group?

_____

_____

_____

Now what factors do you believe need to be present in any productive group?

_____

_____

_____

The following list contains comments made by students in a previous training group:

- The goals of the group were very clear.
- People worked well together.
- There was a sense of belonging among members.
- Everyone took some responsibility to make the group work.
- People communicated directly and openly with each other.
- People listened and respected each other.
- New ideas and creative suggestions invigorated the group.
- Roles and responsibilities were shared and interdependent.
- Differences were confronted and resolved.

Identifying the qualities of an effective group is the starting point for developing awareness and applying this knowledge to a better understanding and functioning of all kinds of groups.

Advantages of Groups

There are many situations and purposes for which forming a group is the preferred method for assisting students. Groups offer a convenient way to provide information and education to several people at the same time. Groups serve as places where opinions can be shared, ideas collected, and problems solved. Groups concentrate the collective energy of several people, allowing them to pool resources and complete a desired task. Peer educators are frequently asked to work with groups in areas such as orientation, advising, health information, and support services that focus on special needs of students. You are most likely being trained along with other prospective peer educators who receive information, hold discussions, interact as a team, and provide support for each other in a group.

In college settings people come together to make social contact for play, fellowship, work, and learning. While the utility of using groups for a variety of educational, recreational, social, or vocational activities is well understood, there is also the prospect of using the group setting for personal growth, self-awareness, and changing individual behaviors. Peer educators can play an important role in facilitating group environments that promote a positive atmosphere where personal growth and learning are most likely to occur.

Yalom (1995) describes eleven factors that can operate within a group to support and facilitate beneficial personal growth. The following discussion synthesizes many of these factors.

When experiencing the self-disclosures of others, people can gain a sense of universalization, realizing that no one is alone in facing the problems and dilemmas in the world. On an emotional level, people may gain qualities of support from a group, such as a sense of belonging, respect, caring, and hope. Positive group experiences demonstrate to the individual the importance of relationship factors such as trust, warmth, understanding, belonging, and community.

Additionally, group interaction can provide personal learning by way of other people through sharing information, imitating successful behavior, gaining direct feedback, or by direct suggestions. Interpersonal learning is an advantage that groups afford by being a laboratory for social interaction. Trying out new behaviors in a social context evokes reactions from others, providing an opportunity for learning in a way that is often parallel to the pattern of social transactions learned with family or friends in the past. Also, one's own perception of self may be validated—or confronted—by the sense of congruence or discrepancy revealed through interaction with others.

A Group Is a System

Of course, not all groups manage to provide the advantages described in the preceding section. Any group is a system, a complex
set of interactive variables that may vary from healthy to unhealthy,
growth enhancing to growth inhibiting. You can usually tell at once
that something is wrong when you experience symptoms of a poorly
functioning group—apathy, boredom, conflict, indifference, frustration, nonsupport, or inability to accomplish purpose. Because the
group is a system, you can compare the function of the group to that
of any organism you assess from both a holistic perspective and an
analysis of the parts.

There are at least ten identifiable features that characterize a collection of people as a group (Cartwright and Zander, 1968). Group
members engage in frequent interaction, define themselves as members, are defined by others as belonging, share norms of behavior on
matters of common interest, participate in a system of interlocking
roles, identify with one another, find the group rewarding, pursue
interdependent goals, have a collective perception of their unity,
and tend to act in a common manner toward their environment.

One way to understand the overall function of a group is to draw
an analogy to the human organism and to check the functioning of
this organism, the group, in the way a medical professional might
conduct a checkup (Newton and Rieman, 1978). As an individual,
you are an entity that at any given point in time may be healthy,
growing, and improving or may be ill, shrinking, or deteriorating.
If you are healthy you might be taking steps to maintain your health
and prevent problems from occurring—taking vitamins, getting exercise, talking to supportive friends, eating right, and having regular
checkups—or you might be accepting your health as a gift and acting in ways that will eventually destroy it. It is quite productive to
view groups through a similar assessment of group health. The following section offers a way for you to conduct a checkup on any
group in which you may participate.

Group Communication

Communication is the cornerstone of social interaction. Within any system, communication is a two-way process connecting one person with another to transmit ideas, experiences, feelings, or intentions. One aspect of the process is the ability to deliver (*encode*) a message. The second important part is to receive and understand (*decode*) the message. Personal factors that interfere with communicative accuracy are ambiguity and other failures in clarity, conflicting nonverbal signals, and interfering thought processes. There are many factors within the environment that may interfere with the communication process. Distractions of *noise*, both visual and auditory clutter, can interfere with reception of a message. Additionally, in a group, multiple conversations and different status levels of the speaker affect the quality of listening—most people tend to listen more carefully to a leader, a friend, or someone they respect highly than to someone they perceive as lower in status than themselves or otherwise dislike or disrespect. Even distractions caused by meeting in a room in which the seating, temperature, or lighting is not comfortable may hamper the attentiveness of group members.

Success in communication may be measured in several ways. One way is to recognize the overlap in message between the communicator and the receiver. This overlap identifies the amount of shared meaning within the transmitted ideas, experiences, feelings, and intentions. The greater the percentage of message that is received, the higher the understanding of those facets of meaning (that is, ideas, feelings, experience, and intentions). Another form of assessment examines the quality of the received message, as it may range from very superficial and insignificant to very important and personally relevant. A third area of assessment includes the pattern of communication between and among group members, pointing out phenomena such as who speaks to whom, how often, and with what level of influence or credibility.

Exercise 1: Group Communication

The purpose of this activity is for you to assess your ability to observe and distinguish how well communication is taking place in a group in which you are participating. First, identify one specific group in your life that relies upon communication for its success. This group could be as informal as a collection of friends who regularly go out to dinner together, or a study group that gathers to prepare for a class project, or, perhaps, an executive board for a student organization that meets to plan an agenda. After you have identified this target group, read the six questions at the end of this exercise and, to the best of your ability, provide a response based upon your observation.

You may well find it quite difficult to frame complete answers to these questions based solely on memory and recall of your experience with the group. A useful alternative is to take an observer notebook with the six questions outlined to the next gathering of the group you have identified, and answer each question as you observe. Your answers will serve as a good pre-test or demonstration of what you do observe and, also, those factors you have missed.

1. After observing a conversation do the following:
    If two circles represented the sender and receiver of a communication, what would be the percentage of overlap (meaningful communication) between them?

    _____

    _____

    _____

    _____

2. What are the sources of communication loss in the group? Consider distractions in the environment as well as problems with the sender and receiver.

_____

_____

3. How clear and specific are the expressions of the sender?

_____

_____

4. How well does the receiver attend to verbal and nonverbal cues?

_____

_____

5. What is the depth of communication taking place? Think of a scale running from 1 (very superficial—things someone would be willing to yell about on a street corner) to 5 (very significant—revealing very personal information).

_____

_____

6. If you were to draw a diagram, what would be the pattern of who speaks to whom, when, and how often?

_____

_____

_____

Group Atmosphere

Atmosphere refers to the tone of the group and may be observed in groups as a positive or negative energy. Atmosphere includes factors such as level of interest, motivation, and commitment of members. This will be reflected in the amount of investment in the group.

Symptoms of high, positive energy include physical activity (talk, animation, doing) directed toward the group, good attendance at meetings or group activities, arriving on time, attentiveness to group tasks, expression of personal feelings, and conversations that stay on group-relevant themes. Low or negative symptoms might be exemplified by attitudes that show indifference, energy directed away from the group, distractions or diversions to outside activity, suppression or concealment of emotions, denial of group importance, poor attendance at meetings and group activities, and tendencies for members to arrive late or leave early.

The most influential factor that affects group atmosphere is cohesion. *Cohesion* is a multidimensional construct that is composed of variables such as attractiveness, tolerance, unity, acceptance, support, belonging, involvement, and even affection. The most distinguishing characteristic of cohesive factors is the shared and mutual perception within the group representing the sense of togetherness and a feeling of belonging to the group (Fuhriman and Burlingame, 1990).

Exercise 2: Group Atmosphere

Think about a group of friends, a study group, or a club or organization in which you regularly attend functions—perhaps the group you identified for Exercise 1. Answer the following questions to assess the type of group atmosphere that prevails and the level of cohesiveness present in your identified group. If you are being trained as a peer educator in a group situation, a second option could be to assess the group atmosphere that has developed to this point with other peer educators.

1. What signs of energy (activity, engagement) do you observe in the group?

   _____

   _____

2. Is the energy positive (supportive, encouraging, full of lively discussion) or negative (argumentative, bored, avoiding the issues)?

_____

_____

3. Do individuals identify and communicate a sense of belonging to the group or of distancing away from the group? Describe this behavior.

_____

_____

4. How do individual members express feeling (verbally or nonverbally) in the group? What do the expressions of feeling reveal?

_____

_____

_____

Normative Behavior

An important facet of group life is how well the group as a whole is able to identify and designate goals, to perform routine functions such as decision making, and to carry out its tasks. Several essential processes influence the group's task functioning. Initially, a group must establish strong, well-understood, yet flexible norms of behavior. Some norms are formally prescribed by agreed-upon standards, such as constitutions and by-laws, but the most important impact of group norms will come from informal yet tacitly understood expectations for how the group will interact. Norms may include such behaviors as starting time, where people sit, when people speak up, the manner in which they speak, and even the style of clothing that they wear.

Because norms are often implicit, unwritten, or unspoken, people who enter any group are initially uncertain about the expectations for behavior and may feel the anxiety and discomfort that naturally result from dealing with an unknown. An important task for any new member of a group is to figure out the appropriate way to behave in that group and gain the practical understanding to function comfortably. For any new group an initial function is to negotiate, oftentimes imperceptibly, the rules for how the group will interact. This sometimes involves controversy over preferences and could result in a vying between factions for a preferred way of act-ing within the group.

The initiation and acceptance of a norm into a group may be il-lustrated by the analogy of planting a seed. Initially, the seed of a new norm is to suggest an idea for a group behavior. This suggestion is made with caution and at times greeted with skepticism—"why do we need this?" If the seed begins to sprout, the young idea may have to compete for space, recognition, and even the nutrients of support necessary to grow into a full-fledged norm. If the norm manages to overcome early resistance, it will grow to become a more frequent behavior of the group, one whose maintenance is reinforced and en-couraged. There may even be pressure for those who do not observe the norm to conform and accept this behavior. Maturation of the norm is clear when the behavior occurs frequently and without ques-tion or dispute by group members. At this point, the norm seems to be a natural part of the group's routine manner of functioning.

Decision-Making Processes

An important facet of norm formation is the decision process. There are several ways that groups can make decisions. Decisions will vary by degree of authority and formality of procedure. A highly autocratic procedure would permit the individual with the greatest status (by position, seniority, or other determining factor) to dictate the deci-sion. A highly democratic procedure might use formal methods such as voting or informal methods such as consensus making that seek input from all members. There are certain advantages and disadvan-tages for each method. A more autocratic method is typically faster and more clear-cut. It tends to work well for urgent or time-pressed situations, though its quality is limited to that of the knowledge of the authority. A more democratic procedure generates a greater resource of knowledge, potentially heightens commitment of members to a decision, and allows the airing of differing opinions and issues about a decision.

Groups may use different decision methods for resolving a variety of group issues. For example, a social group might vote on whether or not to hold a party, conduct a group discussion on the party theme, designate individuals or call for volunteers to take charge of specific tasks, and then authoritatively be told a set budget by the budget administrator. The key to decision success is fitting the right process to the type of decision, the time allotted, and the level of importance for group input.

Conformity

The impact of group norms and group behavior may create pressure to conform and prevent deviations. A group needs a critical balance between maintaining predictability and innovation, between consistency and the infusion of new ideas, and between stability and vitality. If a group develops too strong a tendency toward conformity, it may overlook problems and act prematurely based upon the desire to have a common agreement.

Exercise 3: Group Norms

Your response to these questions will help increase your ability to perceive norm-formation and decision-making processes. Think back to one of the groups that you identified in the preceding exercises for the first two questions, which concern formal group norms.

1. If you were to help a new member gain savvy in a group to which you belong, what four or five rules

of behavior would you give to help the new person
be "in the know"?

_____

_____

_____

_____

_____

2. Identify two or three examples of innovative or
   unique behaviors that represent the possibility of
   new norms that are forming (planting or sprouting
   stage). These examples are characterized by being
   tentative, suggestive, and evoking reactions (for or
   against) from members.

   _____

   _____

   _____

3. Recall the last time you were with a group of
   friends and were trying to decide what to do for the
   evening. How did the group make this decision?
   Describe the methods used, noting especially the
   level of member participation and the degree of
   formality in making the decision.

   _____

   _____

   _____

   _____

   _____

Membership and Roles

There are two levels of membership in a group—joining up and
then making a commitment to it and becoming involved. Joining
occurs when a person is willing to try out a group, wants the status

or favor of association, or sees joining the group as a corollary of a personal goal or commitment. An individual who initiates contact with a group goes through the necessary steps to join, but may still withhold personal energies and avoid engaging completely in group activity. Eventually, if the group proves to be a good match, the individual makes a commitment to participate and begins to invest time, energy, and resources toward the group purpose. A personal level of contribution will take on the distinctive form that suits the personality of the individual, influenced by the degree of personal engagement, and usually fits a niche within the group structure. For example, you may sit in a class every day, take notes, verbally interact only when questioned by the instructor, and fall asleep during lectures. While you have joined the class so as to gain necessary credit in order to receive a degree, your participation is minimal and might be described as that of a passive student. In another situation, you may have voluntarily joined a sports club. You meet for practice on a daily basis, organize many of the practice schedules, socialize with teammates after games, and eagerly seek responsibility as a leader. You have joined this group and are engaged at a high level of activity reflected by a personal pattern or form described as a role.

Membership roles are a way to understand how individuals fit together in a group. Observing a sports team, the functional roles are clearly identifiable. For example, a baseball team has players in positions with very distinct characteristics (pitcher, catcher, fielder). However, in addition to the defined positions and their responsibilities, the players have individual characteristics that describe what they personally bring to the game. Terry is the take-charge player who yells out plays to the rest of the team, while Sam says little but is a tireless worker in all team drills. Similarly, in any group people will take on roles that fit their personality and allow them to fill a niche or function that is important to the group.

Some of these roles may seem to be supportive and necessary for the group's success, others may seem neutral or insignificant, while still others may block or interfere with the group's function. What follows is a list of generalized descriptions of member roles in a group. (Although these generalizations serve the useful purpose of defining types of member interactions, be cautious about applying them in practice—people's actual behavior always has an individual basis that may resemble the stereotype but is not defined or governed by it.)

Individual role-functioning in groups is often broken down into two areas: task functioning and maintenance functioning (Hershey and Blanchard, 1977). Some of the following characterizations are adapted from Posthuma's (1996) description of member roles. Examples of task roles include the *initiator* of ideas and information, the *opinion seeker* who clarifies and elicits ideas from others, the *coordinator* who links together inputs from different sources, the *critic* who evaluates the worth of a strategy or idea, the *synthesizer* who brings together divergent ideas into a coherent whole, and the *energizer* who stimulates the group to take action.

The maintenance functions will operate to support the way a group works together to accomplish tasks with less direct reference to the particular topic or theme that is the target of the group's work. Group maintenance functions could include roles such as the *harmonizer* who attempts to reduce tensions and differences of opinion, the *encourager* who supports other members in the course of participation with the group, the *observer* who may serve as an objective reflector on what is happening in the group, the *gatekeeper* who facilitates involvement by members, and the *doer* who acts without need for recognition to get the job done.

Roles that can thwart or inhibit a group are adopted by people who often act out of their own needs or personality without regard for the group. Characteristics of these members could include the *comedian* who uses humor in ways that can distract the group from its task, the *attention seeker* who—through loud or dominating sorts of behavior—diverts attention from group activities, the *blocker* who seems to resist every idea or effort by being negative or resistant, the *victim* who strives to get rescued or sympathy by self-deprecating statements, and the *bully* who attempts to coerce others to obey rather than work out what is best for the group.

—————

Exercise 4: Membership Roles

Once again, think back to one of the groups you have identified for preceding exercises. If you are participating in a group training session, this exercise is particularly well adapted to apply to that group.

1. What three or four behaviors do you observe in the group supporting the accomplishment of a specific group task? Describe the characteristics of people showing these behaviors and give a label that communicates their role.

    _____

    _____

    _____

    _____

2. Find evidence of distracting, disruptive, or other unproductive individual behaviors. Describe and label these as roles in the same way as for the preceding question.

    _____

    _____

    _____

    _____

—————

Reflection Point 2

Consider your training group, or—if you're studying alone—another group you are participating in:

What role (or roles) do you carry out in this group?

_____

_____

_____

So what are the implications of this role to support positive group interactions?

_____

_____

_____

Now what are some additional role behaviors you could initiate that would contribute to the overall functioning of your training group?

_____

_____

_____

_____

Stages of Development and Group Maturation

All groups go through different stages of maturation that influence the way they operate, and will in many ways determine the group needs and behaviors that are foremost at any given time. Just as an individual develops from a dependent child state through rebellious teen years, matures into responsible adulthood, and then declines toward death, a group will also progress from infancy to dissolution. Several theorists have studied group development, and Table 6.1 generalizes some of the common characteristics noted in groups at key stages. As with definitions of individual roles, however, it is useful to take the table with a grain of salt. Group development does tend to follow a sequence, with certain behaviors being more prevalent at certain times, but behaviors can overlap between stages and the characteristics of any stage can be repeated over again at different times in a group. The table presents more of a template—a list of tendencies and probabilities designed to help you understand group maturation—than an exact map of group developmental functioning.

The important thing about understanding the developmental level of a group is to recognize that different factors or issues will be in the foreground for a group to resolve at a particular stage of maturation. Consider the analogy of individuals' learning a new social interactive game. They must first understand the rules of the game and attain the basic skills of performance. Next, the participants must figure out how to fit together, know what the individual roles will be, and find ways to coordinate with one another. When the initial practice sessions are complete, the participants in the game must work together and find ways to improve or correct mistakes so as to be ultimately productive. Finally, the participants may become proficient as a team. However, to maintain proficiency, the team must find ways to replenish, replace, or terminate the game.

Exercise 5: Stages of a Group

Since this section is asking you to reflect upon groups at different points in their development, anchor your responses for these questions by making general reflections on your overall experience as a group member.

1. What are common emotions experienced by individuals when they first enter a group? How are these feelings resolved?

   _____

   _____

   _____

   _____

   _____

2. What would be four or five characteristics of a group that has matured to the work stage? Give an

Table 6.1.   Stages of Group Development.

Stage	Characteristics	Behaviors for Group
1. Entering	Acquainting, Orienting, Exploring, Testing	• Make relevant self-disclosure • Establish positive atmosphere • Determine initial norms • Link interactions of members
2. Sorting	Initiating, Disagreeing, Compromising	• Recognize individual differences • Overcome dependence • Develop acceptance of conflict • Resolve doubts and difference
3. Cohesiveness	Identification, Organizing, Harmonizing	• Acceptance of group identity • Establish individual roles • Develop commitment and involvement • Determine procedures of operation
4. Working	Resolving, Doing, Achieving	• Make group decisions • Coordinate efforts • Disseminate leadership • Resolve problems • Achieve designated goals
5. Renewal	Maintaining, Evaluating, Restoring, Changing	• Reassess group purpose • Renew commitment • Confront new issues • Resist stagnation, invigorate • Consider dissolution and termination

Source: Adapted from Newton, F. B. "Community Building Strategies with Student Groups." In F. Newton and K. L. Ender (eds.), *Student Development Practices: Strategies for Making a Difference.* Springfield, Ill.: Thomas, 1980, p. 89. Reprinted courtesy of Charles C. Thomas, Publishers, Springfield, Ill.

example of a time you have experienced when a group has worked well and succeeded.

_____

_____

_____

_____

_____

3. Identify three or four characteristics of a group that has stagnated and seems to have grown old. What are a few suggestions that you would make to have the group evaluate and possibly invigorate its stance?

_____

_____

_____

_____

_____

Factors That Promote Group Health

The diagnostic questions about group levels of functioning presented in the preceding sections form a set of tools that will help you support a group's continued well-being. As a diagnostician you need to identify the symptoms of both health and dysfunction—and then know and apply methods to promote and maintain healthy group functioning.

The following sections suggest ways for a group to resolve its problems, seek interventions to change unhealthy procedures, and help promote productive functioning. This information provides some tips and strategies that have the potential to improve a group. These suggestions are only a sample of the possibilities that may be applied in any unique situation—they will give you a start, but the important thing is to stay alert and in touch with the group itself.

Communication

Communication skills are the cornerstone of social interaction. Communicating is the means to link and coordinate one part of the group, a person, to another individual or collective unit. If communication is not facilitating healthy group interaction, an intervention to improve these skills may be necessary.

Tips for Improving Communication Processes

1. Clarify messages.
2. Support group understanding of its direction and purpose.
3. Paraphrase what other members have said.
4. Encourage questions.
5. Share feelings and intentions with others in the group.
6. Personalize messages by saying "I" and "me" instead of "you" or "everybody" when giving your opinions and reactions.
7. Be aware of personal congruence between verbal and nonverbal expressions.
8. Make sure that the group meeting space doesn't offer physical barriers and distractions that reduce the effectiveness of communications.

Group Atmosphere

Symptoms of high positive energy include physical activity, talk, animation, and activities directed toward the group such as good attendance, punctuality, attentiveness, expression of feelings, personally relevant discussion, and cohesive behavior. Low energy symptoms might include indifference, activity directed away from the group, distractions and diversion to competing activity, suppression or concealment of emotions, poor attendance, tardiness, and premature departures.

Tips for Promoting a Positive Group Atmosphere

1. Encourage clarification and direction of activity toward meaningful goals.

2. Confront symptoms of negative energy to promote honest discussion regarding reasons for occurrence. For example, if people arrive late, discuss the behavior and determine if changes need to be made.

3. Encourage individuality and expression of personal opinion while linking those thoughts to the group's overall goals.

4. Recognize accomplishment of cooperative and supportive behaviors.

5. Model behavior that demonstrates willingness to try out new ideas, listen to other possibilities, and make adaptations to improve the way the group operates.

Group Task Behavior

An important facet of group life is how well the group works together to accomplish tasks. Having clear, functional norms, adequate decision-making processes, and conflict management and problem-solving strategies facilitates group performance.

Tips for Helping the Group Stay on Task

1. Make sure that norms are clear and understood, yet flexible and adaptable to changing needs.

2. When a conflict or crisis arises, suggest ways to openly express the difference without resistance or defensiveness.

3. For effective decision-making processes consider context variables such as the type of decision, the time available, the expertise of leaders and members, and the amount of involvement necessary for a good choice.

4. Strive for win-win resolution of differences; avoid defining positions as wholly right or wrong.

5. Be aware of healthy and unhealthy ways of disagreeing. Healthy disagreement produces clear distinctions of different opinions and ideas. Unhealthy disagreement produces reaction and defensiveness in ways that create emotional reactions rather than rational choice.

6. When making group decisions, support clear statement of problems, concise understanding of alternatives, criteria for prioritizing choices, and understanding of group resources.

Coordination of Activity

Coordination is concerned with how well the individual members maintain their uniqueness yet contribute to the total group in a way that moves the group toward its intended goals.

Tips for Improving the Group's Synergy and Ability to Act in Concert

1. Help group members express the desirable consequences of participating as an individual member of the group.

2. Have the group take time to assess the way individuals work together. Make sure the discussion avoids being judgmental and refrains from scapegoating or other individualized put-downs. Constructive criticism will focus on how to make improvements.

3. Support periods of creativity when new ideas and suggestions can be made, experimentation encouraged, and goals reassessed.

4. Encourage expression of both individual feelings and personal impressions of a collective accomplishment.

Exercise 6: Group Synergy

Identify any group in which you are or have been a member. Imagine this group as a giant oak tree. (If this metaphor doesn't appeal to you, pick another—a building, a

garden, an automobile, a sand castle—anything that reflects many diverse qualities.) As a tree . . . consider the
roots, trunk, leaves, access to water, sun, soil, size, age, location, and other qualities. Pose questions such as the following about your metaphor: What parts of the tree
demonstrate the strengths of the group? What parts of the
tree may be deficient? How could the tree grow and improve? Use the analogy to make suggestions on how this
group could change, improve, or maintain its present state.

_____

_____

_____

_____

_____

_____

_____

_____

Maturation

The needs of a young child will vary greatly from those of a teenager,
a young adult, a middle-aged person, or a retired person. It is useful
to consider a group from a similar perspective by attending to needs
at the five levels of group development illustrated in Table 6.1.

Tips for the Entering Stage

1. Find ways to become acquainted and get to know something
   about other group members through self-disclosing and
   demonstration of interest in others.

2. Have means for members to share expectations and interests
   in the group.

3. Ask members to express what they personally hope to gain by
   being in the group and how they would like to interact.

Tips for the Sorting Stage

1. Seek clarification of group purpose and direction.

2. Openly suggest means and methods for how the group will operate (establish common ground rules).

3. Encourage and appreciate various opinions and inputs from people.

Tips for the Cohesiveness Stage

1. Develop a badge of identity such as a name, a logo, or a set of common characteristics.

2. Recognize the norms that group members agree to follow.

3. Show acceptance of unique characteristics and contributions by individuals.

Tips for the Working Stage

1. Make use of problem-solving methods to help the group achieve its goals.

2. Gather ideas and disseminate duties to involve members in a system of complementary, interacting roles and responsibilities.

3. Consider ways to adapt and change when new situations occur.

Tips for the Renewal Stage

1. Hold retreats and have training sessions or reviews to look at ways to assess and potentially change the group.

2. Celebrate completion of goals and make decisions regarding how the group wants to carry on, or possibly dissolve.

3. Determine what it would be like to start over, reinvent the group in a new direction, or maintain the status quo.

Summary

Much of your life is spent as a series of interactions with groups of people. These groups vary in levels of effectiveness (how well people work together to accomplish their purposes) and satisfaction of members (how much cohesiveness develops to motivate a commitment to be involved with group activity). Various dynamics operating within a group are identified as process factors. These include communication, norm formation, member interaction roles, motivation, group cohesion, decision-making strategies, task accomplishment, and maturation level. The chapter has provided you with ways to heighten awareness of group process and make appropriate diagnosis as to how the group is functioning. Subsequently, members can use awareness to make choices, influence change, and generally move a group toward more productive outcomes.

A healthy group becomes a resource for providing information, sharing knowledge, accomplishing tasks, and enhancing personal learning that can be an advantage over individual contact methods.

Chapter Six: Summary Questions

1. What are the advantages to assisting students in a group over working with them as individuals?

2. Identify what is meant by process factors. Define what *norms, communication patterns, group atmosphere, cohesiveness, roles, decision processes,* and *task accomplishment* mean.

_____

_____

3. Groups are characterized by going through stages of development. In your own words, describe two or three predominant
characteristics of a group at each stage.

_____

_____

_____

_____

_____

4. How can a greater awareness of group process enhance or improve the effectiveness and productivity of any group?

_____

_____

_____

_____

_____

_____

7

Leading Groups Effectively

Learning Objectives

After completing this chapter the peer educators will be able to

1. Identify strengths and weaknesses regarding personal qualities and competencies to lead group activity.

2. Distinguish different styles of leader behavior and determine in what situations each style can be most effective.

3. Have knowledge of at least four theories prominent in the past fifty years for describing and explaining leadership behavior.

4. Identify five practices found to be common to successful leaders.

5. Apply a leader planning process for working with a group that includes steps from initiation to evaluation.

6. Understand and employ specific leader strategies to work with groups in particular tasks or situations.

Researchers discuss the concept of leadership endlessly. However, few people who enter positions of authority receive any formal training or preparation to become a leader. As a peer educator, you will probably be asked to accomplish leadership tasks with groups of students. These tasks may include giving presentations, facilitating discussions, helping students work together to complete a project, or perhaps planning a social function. Additionally, when serving or assisting others, you may play a significant role in the development of positive group norms that facilitate self-exploration by permitting members to engage in meaningful and purposeful interaction.

At various times you may be called upon in a group to inspire, motivate, mediate, moderate, support, demonstrate, structure, reflect, or evaluate. Depending on the present needs of the group, you may be very much in charge and at the center of the group activity, or you may find you will serve best by staying in the background and permitting group members to assume their own responsibility and authority. Some knowledge and principles of group leadership will be helpful in looking at your strengths and developing skills as a group leader.

Historical Perspective

What makes a good leader? This is a question that people have been asking for hundreds of years. One early explanation was the "Great Man" theory, which described qualities of superiority displayed by certain very elite individuals who would naturally rise to the top. Another theory was the "Zeitgeist," which explained leadership as a result of situational determinants, such as time, place, and circumstance. A leader emerged because of conditions present that matched the qualities of a person available to take control.

The study of people in organization during the middle part of the twentieth century began to systematically investigate and understand how leadership occurs and how a leader affects group outcomes. A classic study was the comparison of autocratic, democratic, and laissez-faire methods of Boy Scout leaders on group life and individual behavior of children. White and Lippitt (1968) found that autocratic leaders created more dependence, aggressiveness, and discontent among group members, democratic leaders facilitated a more friendly, group-centered, creative, and moderately efficient membership, while laissez faire leadership resulted in detached members producing less work of poorer quality.

Other researchers focused on the impact of task and relationship dimensions on group performance. The *task dimension* emphasized activity for the production of an outcome, such as structuring, decision making, delegating, and the elements of work. The *relationship dimension* was a parallel emphasis on what has been called maintenance, relationship, and process. Studies following these theories compared leader characteristics on the task and relationship dimension with the performance of groups serving different functions. Fiedler (1967) concluded from these studies that the interface of leader style with a group situation would have varying results based on group needs and context, indicating that appropriate leader style was contingent on the situation. Task-oriented leaders performed best in less favorable situational structures. For example, a group facing a time-pressed decision such as organizing to respond to an emergency functioned best with a task-oriented leader. Relationship-oriented leaders responded best in moderately structured situations. The conclusion followed that leaders must adapt their emphasis to the situation, or an appropriate leader must be matched to the right situational task.

Subsequent research has considered several variations to the leadership situation theme. Hershey and Blanchard (1977) added a dimension of group maturation, indicating that task and relationship dimensions will alter with the life cycle of a group. At earlier stages, a group will be more dependent on the leader's structure. As the group matures, members will assume more responsibility and need less leader input. The pattern of leader behavior may move along a continuum from dictating (telling) to persuading (selling), from facilitating (participating) to involving (delegating). House and Mitchell (1974) emphasized the motivational factors of leader behavior, noting the key to leadership as facilitating the "path" of persons to a "goal." The leader's motivational function is to reduce the obstacles and enhance the satisfactions for members to reach a goal. Herzberg (1968) distinguished motivation as having many levels, pointing out that it is necessary to ascertain the difference between direct, extrinsic motivators such as money and personal benefits and indirect, intrinsic motivators such as pride in accomplishment, personal satisfaction, learning, and growth.

Finally, no overview of leadership theory would be complete without consideration of James McGregor Burns's study of significant national and international leaders from the past. Burns (1978) concluded that true leadership is a dynamic and reciprocal exchange between leaders and followers. At the most basic level, the interaction is a transaction to meet a need. The basic exchange may resemble the common phrase, "You scratch my back and I'll scratch yours"— as in a politician's "you vote for me I'll support your issues" promise. However, as people evolve, leadership also may evolve to higher levels. Burns says that the highest level is when a leader can recognize the followers' striving toward personal fulfillment and can both inspire confidence and stimulate followers' action to master more and more complex tasks. Burns mentions Gandhi, Martin Luther King, and John F. Kennedy as examples of inspirational and transformational leaders.

A recent commentary on leadership, the Drucker Foundation's *Leader of the Future* (Hesselbein, Goldsmith, and Beckhard, 1996), considers, from the vantage point of current experts in the study of leadership, the qualities that will be necessary to lead in the "new age." Leaders in the twenty-first century will be those who can assimilate the complexity, change, diversity, and new technology of their world and still take decisive and appropriate action.

Reflection Point 1

Identify someone you know whom you regard as a good leader—someone who manages and operates within a group in a manner that assists the group to function effectively and successfully:

What qualities, characteristics, or behaviors does this individual possess that contribute to the group's success? (Provide three or four illustrations.)

_____

_____

_____

So what can be concluded from this inductive process (looking at attributes of people identified as successful leaders) that describes qualities that contribute to positive leader behaviors? Go back over the list and identify qualities that you believe are strengths or attributes of your own.

_____

_____

_____

Now what are some other qualities that you would like to possess but believe are undeveloped? Discuss how you could develop or improve in one or two of these undeveloped areas.

_____

_____

_____

_____

Practices of Successful Leaders

Kouzes and Posner (1987) surveyed and directly interviewed more than five hundred leaders of organizations and businesses, asking for characteristics of their "personal best case leadership success examples." They found five practices: challenging the process, inspiring a shared vision, enabling others to act, modeling the way, and encouraging the heart. All these practices were common to successful leaders, and were exemplified and implemented through specific leader behaviors. These practices are not magical or innate to an individual, they include attitudes, procedures, and skills that nearly anyone can learn and emulate.

Leaders Stimulate and Challenge

A successful leader acts not to protect the status quo but to stimulate and challenge a group. Kouzes and Posner described this as *challenging the process*, which occurs when a leader is able to innovate and explore new ways of doing things, and is willing to take risks to assist the group. A problem may be seen as an opportunity and a challenge. Mistakes are accepted as a part of learning, and the process of change is experienced as an adventure. Skills of creativity and problem-solving are important in this practice. A creative thinker seeks many possibilities and is able to look at a familiar situation from a different perspective.

De Bono (1971 [1967]) describes the difference between lateral (creative) thinking and status quo (vertical) thinking. Vertical thinking is analogous to digging a hole. Once you have started, you continue to dig the hole bigger and deeper. Because of the investment of time and commitment of energy, it is very difficult to give up this predictive space even when it is not working to meet one's purpose. To think laterally is to choose a place that is experimental, uncertain, and must call upon the use of attention, imagination, and fluency. De Bono's idea of getting stuck in the "hole of familiar patterns" is often referred to as "tunnel vision," or an inability to see new alternatives. For example, many groups follow a set of rules and procedures because "that's the way it has always been done," even when the rationale for the customary way of acting is no longer known. A successful leader knows when to question routine and get the group to act with relevance to the present set of circumstances and group purpose.

It is not necessary for a leader to be the source of every new idea nor to provide the ingenuity for every shift in direction. Rather, the leader can be a facilitator of creative process, using strategies such as asking provocative questions (what if?), setting up experiments, and involving people in retreats, brainstorming sessions, or even art exercises that elicit more right-brain ideas. A leader promotes challenge and change by rewarding those who make suggestions and seek new possibilities. Because the change to new or different ways of doing things will initially heighten anxiety by venturing into the unknown, a leader must demonstrate that the stress of change can be managed and is an acceptable part of the stimulation for something new to happen. Finally, an important function of the leader is to help a group determine which of the new options and possibilities are truly good and useful ideas to follow. A healthy person and a well-functioning group both have the imagination to create, the courage to change, the resilience to recover from a mistake, and the excitement to continue into uncharted areas.

Leaders Activate Focus and Goal Direction

Promoting and directing a group to clearly identify its mission and purpose is an important leader responsibility. Kouzes and Posner (1987) referred to this as *inspiring a shared vision*. The idea of a vision is to release the imagination of a group to venture from the present moment to take a look into the future, and to go from a starting point to speculate what it would be like when reaching a destination. For example, when a teacher begins a class discussion period, the first question could be, "When you leave this class period, what would you like to have accomplished?" It is not sufficient for a leader to impose a goal on the rest of the group members. Successful leaders engage followers in a manner that elicits the personal commitment and energy of each member toward some shared ends. The goals of all members need not necessarily be the same, but there must be a mutual acceptance that all can benefit from the interaction and cooperation of the group activity.

The task of inspiring a vision implies that a leader must have the tools of a visionary. Being a visionary means to make use of the experiences of the past (knowing the pluses and the minuses, the strengths and the weaknesses), to identify the needs and purposes of a group at the present, and to be able to look into the future—seeing the possibilities, both ideals and potentials. To have a shared vision is to pool together the collective possibilities of a group so as to have room for both the unique aspirations of individuals and the mutual considerations of the larger identity.

There are certain ways that a leader may communicate to promote a future direction. Six factors may be considered as tests that determine the potential for a promising idea to become a shared group commitment.

- *Value or principle*. The idea is important to a core belief of the group membership.

- *Credibility*. The idea is grounded in evidence of its worth.

- *Inclusiveness*. The idea is shared so that all members can be a part of the vision.

- *Clarity*. The idea is communicated with enough illustration to be vivid in the minds of the group members.

- *Positiveness*. The idea is stated in an affirmative way that communicates the hopes and anticipations of members.

- *Passion*. The idea taps the emotions and the hearts of group members, providing a driving force for accomplishing the vision.

Leaders Support Member Involvement

Returning to Kouzes and Posner's practices of successful leaders, the third practice is to *enable others to act*. There is an old Taoist proverb that reads: "That leader is best whom people barely know of, not so good whom people obey and acclaim, and worst whom they despise. Of a good leader who talks little when the work is done and the aims fulfilled, the group will say, 'We did this ourselves.'" The emphasis in the most effective groups is to attain a team or "we" atmosphere in which the commitment and energy of all group members is activated. The activity most central to engaging others is to facilitate cooperative and collaborative behavior.

Leaders Model Effective Behavior

The fourth practice of effective leaders is to set an example for others. Kouzes and Posner (1987) describe it as *modeling the way*. The principle of an exemplary leader emphasizes the importance of action over words. It is the opposite of the parental admonition, "Do as I say, not as I do." Included here are six areas in which leaders can model the way for a group:

- A leader demonstrates behavior that is consistent with a set of values or principles. The leader can clearly identify the principles that a group stands for and then act in ways that will establish, promote, and maintain those values.

- A leader communicates in a manner that is clear, understandable, and up-front. This can be accomplished by stating the purpose and motivation for any group activity or agenda. The leader avoids covert, hypocritical, and ambiguous messages (sometimes referred to as B.S.).

- A leader demonstrates a caring and respectful attitude toward others when in face-to-face contact, and also shows a sense of consideration and dignity for others outside the immediate environment.

- A leader shows engagement and works intently toward completing the tasks of the group. A true leader energizes a group by modeling the commitment and effort needed to make things happen, inspiring the group to establish strong norms for hard work and achievement.

However, to be productive, a leader must also pay attention to counterproductive factors such as job stress, burnout or fatigue, or emotional tension, and work to reduce or prevent them.

- A leader acts to maintain behavior that reflects fair play and integrity and establishes standards for ethical conduct.

- A leader models effectiveness, which may be the single most important action a leader can demonstrate.

Leaders Recognize and Reward

An organization will thrive best when there is recognition both for doing the little things that make a difference and for reaching goals and succeeding in major accomplishments. Sincere acts of unselfish kindness, observations and gestures reflecting interest, and acknowledgment of individual uniqueness are all ways a leader is responsive and encouraging to members. Reinforcement of even small steps toward group goals provides participants with incentive and a sense of progress. Recognition may vary from routine acknowledgments such as "That was a good idea" to regular updates or reports on what individuals have accomplished. Additionally, paying attention to support strategies such as personal messages commemorating birthdays, refreshments at meetings, or responses that reflect individual contributions toward special events are valued incentives to members. On a larger scale, at significant points of the group's life, it is important to have celebrations to note accomplishments such as award ceremonies and "We did it!" parties.

Reflection Point 2

The following activity can be completed individually or with a training group. If completed in the group setting your training leader or teacher will direct you on how a group will undertake this task.

On a large sheet of paper (a piece of newsprint or a section from a paper roll used to cover tables will do), draw a line across the width of the paper that divides the paper in half horizontally along the midpoint. Next, divide the line into three parts and label these parts past, present, and future. Identify a group that you have been actively involved in while a college student. If you are working with a training group you may wish to use this group as the example, although another group can serve the purpose. From the vantage point of the group's history, its present activity, and its possible future direction, identify significant milestones in the life of this group. Locate and label these points chronologically on the time line.

What can you summarize about the purpose, methods, and successes of this group?

_____

_____

_____

_____

So what does the history and present status of the group's functioning have to do with the future possibilities of this group?

_____

_____

_____

_____

Now what steps or measures could a leader take to make it easier for this group to assess and determine future directions?

_____

_____

_____

_____

_____

Practical Tips and Strategies

This section describes many practical strategies that a leader can use to enhance the functioning of a group. While it will read like a cookbook and is indeed meant to provide examples for many specific situations that you may encounter, it will not be an exhaustive compendium of all the strategies that may be needed in a group. As noted for earlier sets of suggestions, these tips are designed as a starting point, not a final answer to every problem.

Building a Cohesive Team

Nearly any group will benefit when members develop a sense of identity and commitment to the group with which they are involved. A sense of team identity may be less important for a group that is coming together briefly to receive or share information. However, even during brief contacts, having a sense of the value, purpose, and common benefit from the experience can increase participant attention and engagement with the task. For a group that will have continued involvement and personal investment over time, the development of a cohesive team atmosphere is essential.

Team building has both personal and group dimensions. It begins when individuals are able to share information about themselves and get to know others in the group on a personal basis. The personal alliances that develop become a basis for positive communication, a working relationship, and a determination of how individual needs, interests, and capabilities will fit into an overall group purpose. The group dimensions are then generated by the manner in which individuals can identify common denominators for determining the goals of the group and the methods in which these goals can be accomplished through member interaction. When members have a strong identity and a sense of belonging with a group, they will have a greater investment in and commitment to group activities.

Tips for Team Building

1. Provide an icebreaking activity soon after the formation of any group so members will gain personal contact with others.

Icebreakers can be as simple as getting the name and shaking the hand of persons sitting next to each other in a lecture. Or, for a group that will interact more closely, they could be more involved and elaborate activities such as sharing values or purpose ("three principles that guide my life") or personal information ("my proudest moment in the past month").

2. Hold an initial session in which group participants join up by going through a process in which they express individual expectations and goals, determine common and complementary interests with other members, and formulate group goals.

3. Demonstrate the significance of cooperative and collaborative effort within the group by providing a simulation, game, or group task. Then have the group members discuss how they were able to interact together. An interactive game using art supplies to build a "product" is an example of a typical group task. More elaborate team-building processes may have a group do skits or role-plays that depict the special qualities of their members and the outcome of their collective identity.

4. After initial stages of team building have been accomplished, take time periodically for the assessment of team interactions. Include a review of how the group communicates, identify team accomplishments, and gather suggestions for the future. Use these times to celebrate collective successes and look for ways to reinvigorate the group and make improvements for the future.

Making Decisions and Accomplishing Tasks

Typically, a group organized to achieve an outcome must make several decisions before organizing and implementing actions necessary for completing a task. The decision process is often the most critical moment in the success of a group goal. The way a decision is made can determine the quality of input given to the decision, the degree of commitment members will hold for carrying out the decision, and the definition provided for organizing members to complete the task.

A leader must attend to three important variables in leading the decision process. The first is to determine ways to define and clarify the question or problem to be decided upon. The second is to determine the manner in which participants will make inputs into the process and come to resolution. The third is to determine how any decision will be implemented through a process of organizing the members to carry through on the decision.

Structuring a group to facilitate the actual implementation of a plan and accomplishment of designated goals is a critical aspect of leadership. It may include strategies for assessing what tasks need to be done and who can do them at the beginning of the process, evaluating how well each task was done, and organizing a celebration of successes at the end. Through this process a leader may seem more like a manager and problem solver. However, while systematic organizational strategies may be followed, the leader will also need the ability to adapt to special needs that arise and the sensitivity to notice and help resolve individual differences that occur.

Tips for Decision Making and Task Accomplishment

1. Clarify the decisions that the group or organization needs to address, stating issues, problem areas, organizational objectives, and the context for needing a decision at a given time.

2. Define the methods for reaching a decision. Decision methods may be clearly defined by formal organizations that have a written set of procedures for inputs and discussion and for making a decision, such as outlined by Robert's Rules of Order. However, most organizations will have less formal decision-making processes that allow for a wide range of involvement and participation from members.

3. Generally, significant decisions of a group that will affect all members and require a strong commitment of participants should follow procedures with high levels of member input. Providing means for open discussion and some form of demo-

cratic resolution will make for better decisions and may be a
necessity for successful group support and accomplishment.

4. Decisions that are less significant, relate to carrying through
   detail, or are subgoals already established by group input can
   be delegated to individuals, committees, or other units given
   the authority to efficiently and expeditiously make an ad hoc
   decision.

5. Be prepared to make decisions for the group at times when
   face-to-face group decisions cannot be made or emergency
   time restraints eliminate the possibility for group input, but
   consider group interests carefully in such decisions.

6. Delegate tasks to group members in a manner that considers
   the individual capabilities, interests, and fit to the job at hand.
   When possible, use voluntary input and self-determination of
   members to guide the process. The more members feel they
   have a clear and definitive role in contributing to a task, the
   greater group involvement will be.

7. Provide job descriptions, task definitions, time parameters,
   and other structure in very clear terms when making delega-
   tions. Follow up decision-making and task delegation sessions
   with written summaries that clarify and reinforce what has
   been determined so that all group members are clearly aware
   of expectations that result.

8. Use checkpoints and follow-up sessions to note progress and
   accomplishments of any group decision.

Impact of Physical Environment

The physical environment can critically influence the nature of activity and the level of performance that a group may achieve. It is
important for a leader to anticipate, when possible, the optimum
conditions of meeting space by planning and arranging space needs.
Consideration should be made for physical comfort (including such
factors as temperature, lighting, seating), freedom from distractions

(noise, competing activity), and seating arrangements appropriate for the tasks of the group.

Tips for Using Space

1. Check out any space that will be used for a group in advance to make arrangements or resolve problems. It is important to know if there is adequate seating arranged in an appropriate way.

2. Make sure that whatever writing surfaces, visual aids, and other supplies the group may need are present or available.

3. Be sure the environment is conducive to the task, including lighting, temperature, and elimination of distractions.

4. Follow up to make sure that any special arrangements or refreshments are ready on time. One of the most inefficient ways to start a meeting or hold any group activity is to waste time and energy by unlocking doors, finding chairs, or locating a resource that could have been taken care of by careful preparation.

When considering seating arrangements, remember that they need to be tailored for the kind of interaction you have in mind. Here are the strengths and weaknesses of the various options:

Theater seating: Row seating is best used for providing information via lecture or similar presentations. A theater format provides good visual contact with the audience for the speaker. It also allows the audience direct visual and sound access to demonstration methods and media aids. However, this arrangement is not good for stimulating discussion or active two-way involvement with participants.

Roundtable seating: A conference room setup permits face-to-face interaction among all participants. This promotes discussions and dialogue between people. Table surface can serve the function of holding materials, notes, or other work tasks, and communicates a business atmosphere.

Horseshoe seating: When the goal is to focus discussion on a project or a problem rather than on the group and its plans, it can be useful to arrange the seating around three sides of a table, with a white-board or flip chart on the fourth side where someone can keep track of points and decisions. This retains the advantages of the round-table setup while diverting members' attention from each other.

Living room–style seating: On the other hand, tables can be a barrier when more informality, interpersonal contact, and participant movement is desired. When you want to establish these latter conditions, set up a casual arrangement with comfortable seating that removes tables and other barriers from the meeting space.

Group Experiences for Interpersonal Growth

One role of peer educators may be the facilitation of support groups or structured experiences in which the focus is to improve personal growth or interpersonal behavior of members. Examples of peer support groups include areas of wellness (exercise, diet), recovery (campus Alanon, Alcoholics Anonymous, eating disorders), self-improvement (overcoming shyness, leadership training), and identity (women in engineering, gay and lesbian students). Whenever the purpose of a group experience includes self-disclosure and self-improvement, it is very important to establish the conditions of safety and support for promoting personal exploration of what most people consider to be private and vulnerable information about themselves. After establishing necessary conditions for allowing personal revelation, it is important to create a helpful atmosphere where open exploration, enhanced personal understanding, and potential growth can occur. In short, a leader has responsibilities for establishing an ambience in which personal information can be safely shared and a process in which self-exploration and discovery can take place.

However, the most important caveat for all peer educators is to recognize that they are not professional counselors. It is essential to establish clear restrictions as to the purpose and limits of any peer group that is initiated with personal exploration and growth as an outcome.

Necessary Conditions for Self-Disclosure

The development of trust is an important prerequisite for people to share information about themselves in a group situation. Trust is a condition earned through demonstration that ensures that the group environment will be safe, accepting, caring, respectful, and honest. While it is often helpful initially to describe these conditions to group members and suggest that they be considered principles that will operate within the group, the trusting environment becomes a reality when the leader and members consistently display the promised behaviors. Group members will initially be cautious and reserved, testing the norms and integrity of the group to ensure that it is a safe place. This is a normal process, so a leader must allow time for testing and confirmation of group norms so that trust can be assured.

A second important condition is the provision of openness. Conventional communication may often contain indirect messages and subtle signs that disguise or hide underlying feelings, motivations, and intentions. The indirect message provides a certain amount of protection from the vulnerability and discomfort of what is usually a very personal form of thinking or feeling. Protection is often used to prevent a feeling of rejection, belittlement, or exposure to a very private side of human nature. Personal learning at a deeper level, however, necessitates that people be open, frank, and candid in their communication with others. This does not mean that a person must reveal every private thought and feeling in a group. However, it does mean that what is chosen for disclosure must be sincere, honest, and clearly communicated.

The third condition for self-disclosure is the presence of effective listening between group members. When people do disclose information about themselves, it needs to be heard. More important, it needs to be understood from the individual speaker's own frame of reference. The development of effective communication and listening skills was discussed in Chapter Four. A leader of a support group may need to promote effective listening and communication skills through instructional activity, good modeling, or interventions that take place based on the evolving dynamic of a group.

Helpful Interacting

A group environment may provide the opportunity for participants to benefit and learn about themselves in ways they could not manage on their own because of conditions that are present only through interaction with others. The following are factors that describe the advantages for personal learning to occur in a group. First, individuals obtain many ideas through the demonstration and example of others' behavior. The observation of another's action provides a role model or simulation activity. This serves both to suggest possibilities and to show strategies that can be applied to one's own life. Similarly, when a person tries out a behavior in a group, the group is apt to provide feedback and reactions—letting the experimenter know how the behaviors came across and offering suggestions on how improvements could be made. The very act of trying out an idea or behavior in a group can bring the validation and support of others, which leads to more confident initiation outside the group.

A group also supports the building of self-acceptance and improved self-esteem. Yalom (1995) describes one of these factors as "universalization." Universalization is explained as an attitude that expresses how people are similar in many ways to others, sharing many of the same problems and insecurities as well as many of the same hopes and dreams for their lives. To know that one is not alone in dealing with the difficulties of life provides both a sense of relief and a prospect of hope. A group also serves as an emotional outlet to release pent-up feelings, to experience the support of acceptance after revealing the inner self, and to receive the internal reward that comes with contributing and giving to others.

Tips for Leading Support Groups

1. Describe clearly to all group members both the purpose and the limitations of the group experience.

2. Provide a discussion of potential ground rules for the establishment of trust, support, and open communication in the group. Allow group members an opportunity to give input and discuss how these guidelines may be implemented.

3. Ask group members to share initial expectations and personal goals for what they would like to accomplish through the group experience.

4. Initiate process interventions within the group to create an open atmosphere where members can share impressions on the communication, trust, and other dimensions of group interaction.

5. Use a problem-solving approach in a manner that emphasizes the positive, such as "What did you like about this group session?" and "What are ways that we, as group members, could improve our listening skills?"

6. Provide a summary or recapitulation of each session that reflects on what has been accomplished and emphasizes the meaning or understanding of the session. Allow group members to make brief summaries of what they learned.

7. Make sure that closure is brought before the completion of any group experience intended for personal growth. Closure should include dealing with unfinished business, which means allowing group members to ask questions or deal with group issues that they feel are incomplete. Closure should also reflect upon the meaning of the experience, what has been learned, and how that knowledge can be used beyond the group. Finally, there should be a time to say good-bye and acknowledge the importance of others.

Special Problems Confronting Peer Educators Leading Groups

Underparticipation by Members

When people are uninvolved with group activity they tend to miss meetings, arrive late, or leave early. However, even without attendance problems, there are other behaviors that show minimal participation and engagement. People who don't feel engaged with a group are apt to be reluctant to speak up or verbally interact, even when opportunities are solicited. They may also allow themselves to be distracted easily from group focus by doing things such as looking out a window, reading a paper, or holding unrelated conversations with a friend. Boredom or indifference may be observed through blank looks, avoiding emotion, and a general lack of energy or engagement shown by physical lethargy and refusal of eye contact.

While the symptoms are clearly observable, the causes of these symptoms may be less certain. The behaviors could signal a lack of clarity and purpose for the group, a feature that may be common during the forming stage of a group but should diminish quickly once the group becomes established. Another cause of apathetic and disengaged behavior is a lack of commitment to a group. Some people will attend or join a situation because it is a requirement or an expectation, but make little personal investment in it. The attitudes of those who are required to take a class they do not like, who join a group with little interest but think it will look "good on the résumé," or are just there because "everybody else is doing it" are instantly recognizable. A third factor includes individual personalities—some people may feel too shy, uneasy, or inexperienced to speak up, show involvement, or make assertive input to group activity even though they actually do care about what the group is doing. Lack of involvement may also reflect problems within the dynamics operating in a group. Some people may be afraid of criticism, making a mistake, being embarrassed, or losing status through their actions. This could be due to group norms that create defensiveness, such as hostile comments or threats, ridicule, disrespectful statements, demonstration of prejudice toward subgroup members, or a sense that no one cares or is interested in the individual. To correct these symptoms, a leader must be able to diagnose the cause and have ways to respond to the appropriate issue.

Tips for Increasing Involvement

1. To facilitate more equal involvement from all types of personalities, shy as well as gregarious, provide simple methods that solicit total participation. For example, have everybody write down an idea, then have each member state their idea by writing it on a chalk board or flip chart. Break down the group into smaller groups to initiate more active participation, perhaps starting with two people and building to smaller face-to-face groups, especially when the group is larger than twelve people.

2. Keep the group focused so that all members know the task, the limits of time, and the need for staying on track to accomplish specific ends. Establish clear and specific norms for when a meeting will start. Adhering to those norms communicates an expectation that they will be followed consistently. Finishing a meeting on time with the task accomplished can be an equally rewarding outcome for good group performance.

3. Challenge a group to make an investment in the activity of the group, so that it becomes a clear and open part of membership that everyone recognizes that their involvement is a high priority and a worthy commitment for the group. When this is done openly, it will challenge the uncommitted to make a decision, and, if not willing to make an investment, they may leave voluntarily.

4. Observe group behaviors that show a lack of involvement. Communicate your observations to the group in an open way,

without indictment or hostility, inviting members to discuss what is going on with the group and what can be done about it. For example, make an observant inquiry such as "The group seems tired and detached today . . . is something going on that we should talk about?" This method of open discussion invites group members to make inputs and possible suggestions as to how the group can be improved.

Conflict Among Members

The good news about the presence of conflict in a group is that it indicates that people are engaged and are willing to provide opinions. It also means that differences of opinion can be aired and that problems can be approached through a reflection upon a diversity of pros and cons and strengths and weaknesses of any idea. The presence of difference and conflict typically leads to feelings of tension. This, again, can be positive, as tension at a certain level will engage and energize a group.

The bad news about conflict and differences is that when it creates factionalization or cliques within a group, members may feel polarized and sometimes alienated. This is especially true when differences are viewed in a win-lose context. It is important to value difference without creating individual defensiveness and to promote scrutiny and critique of ideas and group decisions without attaching the worth or viability of the person to the outcome. The key to dealing with conflict and difference is finding an acceptable process in which differences actually promote better group outcomes without alienating group members.

Tips for Dealing with Conflict

1. Set up ground rules for looking at both sides of any issue. Ground rules should espouse ways to openly discuss differences. Suggesting that the group make a list of both the pros and the cons of any disputed issue can accomplish this goal.

2. Separate the issues from personal attachment. Make sure, as a leader, that tactics that polarize and personalize groups into win-lose situations do not occur. Be clear that hostile tactics are not tolerated—there is no room for defaming statements about individuals ("Your ideas are always bad"), throwing blame at individuals ("If we fail it will be your fault"), or using blackmail ("If this decision is made, don't expect me to be involved").

3. When a decision has been made and a direction determined, be clear to group members that it was important to have had everybody's input and that it is equally important in the future to continue to have everybody's support. Make sure that everyone gains the understanding that even people who oppose the majority's ideas are considered as having valued input now and in the future.

Problem Personalities

There will frequently be people with personalities that may have a negative impact on a group, either by blocking effective group practice or creating interpersonal difficulties. It would be a difficult if not impossible task to identify in this chapter a comprehensive description of the potential types of difficult personalities that one might encounter in a group. However, we can cite a few examples and provide some tips for encountering difficult individuals and responding in general to these situations.

Monopolizers

Groups will often have members who tend to dominate verbally and bring undue attention to themselves. Initially this type of behavior might be a relief to others, as they may believe that it takes responsibility and effort off themselves for group participation. However, it soon becomes apparent that domination by a few will deter a more balanced group participation and limit positive inputs from those who do not wish to compete with an aggressive personality. Deference will lead to many members' showing less interest and becoming annoyed with the domination. A common problem with a domineering type is that leaders and other group members accept the behavior initially and then find it difficult to deal with the monopolizer when the behavior is recognized later as a problem. Reprimanding a person at that point feels inconsistent, as though the initial acceptance set up a sort of contract as to what behavior would be accepted in the future—and the typical monopolizer will be quick to take advantage of any reservations the group or its leader may show.

Manipulators

There are many ways that some people will use to have a sense of control and protection for themselves. One set of strategies this type of person may adopt includes forms of seduction, in which they draw support from others by feigning interest, showing fragility, or attracting attention in an alluring way. Manipulative people often communicate a dependency on others and a need for rescue or support, which makes them particularly difficult to confront.

Distracters

This type of individual may sidetrack a group with behaviors that lead a group off task. They may clown around and use humor to get off the subject, or may just be loud and disruptive by talking to a neighbor while the group is conducting business. Again, these people can be difficult to deal with because they have a good defense response when they retort that "they were just trying to have a little fun."

Aggressors

An angry or attacking person will create considerable disturbance in any group. Confronting such a person will present a challenge or competition for them to fight or debate. On the other hand, to acquiesce and avoid the conflict creates an acceptance of an environment that a hostile bully will dominate. A group will often disintegrate if hostile behavior is allowed to continue.

Harmonizers

Some people will try so hard to please, help others, or create a peace-ful, no-conflict atmosphere that their behavior actually does more harm than good. For example, they may act to gloss over any conflict quickly so as to avoid tensions in a group, thereby short-circuiting issues of difference that may need to be discussed. They also may respond to individuals who appear to need support for a problem. Their typical response attempts to help by overloading the person with suggestions ("Have you tried this . . . or this . . . and this is what I did last year") or provides potentially false reassurance ("Don't feel bad; I'm sure everything will turn out all right").

Tips for Dealing with Problem Personalities

1. Take the initiative by spending some time at the beginning of a group for members to discuss positive ways in which they can interact and be productive.

2. Confront unacceptable behaviors while still demonstrating acceptance of the person. Make it clear that you can be an-noyed, displeased, or angered at a behavior without diminish-ing the person's character. For example, "I appreciate how much energy you show in the group, Terry, but I also observe that your behavior doesn't allow others who are more quiet to have time for input" is likely to get much better results than "Sit down and shut up!"

3. When confronting a person, be factual and explicit about what you observe and how such a behavior affects the group. For example, use a statement such as "I notice that the side conversations taking place are distracting attention from our group activity." Do not use judgmental labeling such as "That was dumb," "You're acting stupid," or "Quit being a baby."

4. Be direct and honest. Do not use satirical remarks or innu-endo to get your point across. "Sandy, your talking on the cell

phone while we are meeting is distracting me" is more tactful than "Sandy, do you have to make that date on group time?"

5. Suggest that group members process their reactions as to how a person's behavior affects the group as a whole by asking members to respond to specific observations. Examples might include such statements as "What are those of you who were silent today thinking and feeling?" or "I sense that many people seemed to back off when Kim got angry at Lee; can we discuss those reactions now and how they may be affecting our interactions?"

6. If certain member behaviors are very destructive and the group is not an appropriate place for discussion of individual behaviors, meet with the individual on a one-to-one basis outside the group setting. Be prepared to suggest alternative behaviors or other options for the individual. However, you still may have to define boundaries of behavior for being a part of the group, which may include a necessary step to suggest severance from the group or organization.

7. If a person's behavior seems to reflect personal issues or trauma in their life, be willing to refer that individual for professional help. Do this in a helpful way that shows concern and interest.

Reflection Point 3

Kouzes and Posner identified five practices of successful leaders. Briefly state what these practices are, then reflect on your own behavior in working with groups:

_____

_____

_____

_____

_____

What practice do you consider to be your strongest, and what do you believe is your weakest?

_____

_____

_____

So *what* effect will your strengths and weaknesses have on the group or groups with whom you are working?

_____

_____

_____

Now *what* do you suggest could be a way to improve your weakness or make better use of your strength?

_____

_____

_____

Summary

There is a wealth of information about how leaders can be most effective in working with groups. In spite of the early theories that a person is born to be a leader or that a leader emerges automatically as the result of special circumstances, there are very clearly identified principles, attitudes, skills, and strategies that can be developed by any individual.

Chapter Seven: Summary Questions

1. At one time, studies of leadership looked at individual traits, problem situations, and group tasks as the variables that determined who could become a leader. More recent emphasis has been placed on leader attitudes, skills, and the ability to engage others in ways that model and motivate participation as a team. Take

a position on whether you believe a "leader is born" or a "leader is made." Explain what implications your position will have on the training and preparation of people for leadership positions.

_____

_____

_____

_____

_____

_____

2. Describe the differences between Burns's description of transactional and transformational leadership. Give an example of a transactional and transformational leader behavior from a group in which you have been a member.

_____

_____

_____

_____

_____

_____

3. Assume that in your role as a peer educator you have been given the assignment to meet with a small group of students in a freshmen residence hall who have been identified from their first set of midterm tests as being at risk for failing their classes. The hall director has sent a letter to these students instructing them to meet with you at a designated meeting time in the next week. Make a list of five or more things (tips) you will do to prepare for initiating this contact with these students. Why did you choose these tips?

_____

_____

_____

_____

_____

4. What are four necessary conditions for establishing trusting and helpful group interactions when leading support groups for personal growth experiences?

_____

_____

_____

_____

_____

8

Strategies for Academic Success

Sally Lipsky

Learning Objectives

After completing this chapter the peer educators will be able to

1. Define study system and active learning.

2. Describe and apply three types of time management schedules.

3. List factors students should consider when scheduling study time.

4. Identify effective study locations as well as ways to reduce or eliminate study distractions.

5. Describe and apply strategies recommended before, during, and after a lecture that result in effective listening.

6. Identify and apply strategies that are linked to more effective and efficient textbook reading.

7. Describe and apply differing types of study guides.

8. List, explain, and use three study techniques that promote effective test preparation.

In this chapter, we will illustrate the concept of a Learner Packet as we present effective study strategies. The Learner Packet represents a self-contained learning module that peer educators can develop and use with students. Typically, the Learner Packet is written to assist students as they work to overcome a skill deficit. Assessment is a tool used extensively in most Learner Packets. We provide this illustration in the area of study strategies, believing that all students with whom you have contact may profit from enhanced study skills, regardless of how effective they already are at studying. Many peer educators are recruited to work in this area, and many others will have occasion to deal with it in the course of other efforts. This chapter introduces concepts of systematic study and time management that peer educators can use in their own classes and model for the students they work with.

Developing a System of Study

A system of study consists of a student's behaviors, attitudes, and learning styles, all integrated into a framework of learning. It includes those habits and strategies that a student employs when tackling day-to-day academic demands. These strategies can vary greatly from student to student, though there are universal behaviors and attitudes that tend to work for most students.

As a peer educator, you will be working with students who may need guidance in developing an efficient and effective system of study. In fact, you may need some assistance in this area to effectively model successful study strategies for others. Some students might need a radical overhaul, that is, a complete restructuring and rethinking of their study systems. For others, it might be a matter of some small changes or fine-tuning of strategies. Either way, change does not come easily; it involves an assessment of weaknesses and strengths and a willingness to take some risks.

This chapter will approach change as an ongoing process consisting of small steps adding up to an integrated whole, that is, a whole system of study that leads students toward academic success. As a method to increase your learning in this area, you will be asked to assess, implement, and evaluate your own system of study.

Passive Versus Active Students

This section describes two students. As you read about these students, note the differences between the two.

The Passive Student

It is nine o'clock on Wednesday evening as Paul, who is in his room, begins studying for tomorrow's German quiz. As he opens his book, the hall counselor knocks on the door and wants to chat about Paul's ideas for upcoming programs in the residence hall. Paul listens to the hall counselor chat about programming ideas and also about his fraternity's mixer this coming weekend. The hall counselor finally leaves Paul's room at 10 P.M. As Paul opens his German book again, he hears loud music blaring from his neighbor's room. Paul covers his ears in an attempt to lessen the distraction of the music, but still has trouble concentrating on the German vocabulary words he needs to know. Ten minutes later Paul's roommate comes in the room and turns on his TV to the nightly *Star Trek* rerun. Paul closes his German book in exasperation and flops on his bed to watch the program.

The Active Student

Sue enters the large lecture hall for her sociology class and begins to walk toward the front. Sue hears her name called out and turns around to see Marjorie, an acquaintance from her swimming class. Marjorie asks Sue to sit with her and her friends. Sue declines the invitation, saying that she will see Marjorie after class. Sue takes her customary seat in the middle of the first row. Sue quickly opens her textbook, noting the question marks she had written the night before next to the material she was unsure of. As her professor lectures on the day's topic, Sue jots down key ideas that the professor seems to be emphasizing. Once, when she was unable to keep up with the professor, Sue raised her hand and asked him to repeat an idea. When the professor reached the information included in the textbook, Sue kept her eyes on her text pages, using her pen to jot down clarifying material in the margins. At the end of the lecture class, Sue approached her professor to tell him that she was still uncertain about some text information. He made an appointment to see Sue for the next day. After jotting the time in her appointment book, Sue ran to find Marjorie.

Exercise 1: Study Differences

Think about the way Paul and Sue study:

What is the difference between Paul's and Sue's study systems?

_____

_____

_____

So what is Paul doing (or not doing) that undermines his attempts at effective studying?

_____

_____

_____

Now what specific changes can you recommend for Paul to become a more active student?

_____

_____

_____

Controlling Your Time

The study area that is the downfall of many college students is time management. It is a novelty to have so much freedom in how they spend their time. Unlike high school, in college classes do not begin and end back to back, teachers and administrators are not checking daily class attendance, and parents are not around to oversee homework and grades. Instead, students can freely choose whether to go to class or watch the soap operas, whether to do calculus homework or go out for pizza with friends. Many times the effects of these choices are not known until grades arrive in the mail.

How about you? Do you generally make productive use of your time? What could you do to more effectively control your time? On the assessment questionnaire in Exhibit 8.1 mark those items that would probably aid you with your college academics; your answers will help you choose what types of schedules would be most effective for you.

Exhibit 8.1. Time Management Checklist.

☐　1. Writing down what assignment is due when.

☐　2. Being able to look at due dates on a calendar.

☐　3. Noting chores and activities to be accomplished.

☐　4. Anticipating how much study time you'll need in an upcoming week.

☐　5. Being able to cross off accomplished activities.

☐　6. Having a ready reference of a week's responsibilities.

☐　7. Carrying around a daily calendar of events.

☐　8. Providing guidelines for how much leisure time you'll use.

☐　9. Writing down what you will study at what time.

☐　10. Putting time limits on study breaks.

☐　11. Prioritizing a day's activities.

☐　12. Providing a general overview of anticipated weekly activities.

☐　13. Providing a structured overview of anticipated weekly activities.

Semester Calendar

If you checked items 1, 2, or 5 on the time management checklist, you will probably benefit from using a semester calendar. Of the three types of written schedules, the semester calendar is the most general, since it only consists of important due dates including exams, quizzes, papers, and assignments written down for each semester. This schedule allows you to plan ahead and pace yourself for the upcoming term. Use the syllabus you receive at the beginning of the term from each instructor to fill in due dates. You'll quickly notice patterns in the semester; that is, you'll see where assignments tend to pile up, typically around midterm and the end of the semester, and where you have some breaks in assignments and exams. Use this schedule to pace your studying throughout the semester.

Weekly Schedule

If you checked items 4, 5, 6, 8, 9, 10, 12, or 13 on the time management checklist, you will probably benefit from using a weekly schedule. The purpose of a weekly schedule is to provide an overview of a week's activities. Consider such a schedule as a guideline for how you anticipate spending your time.

A widely recommended format for a weekly schedule is the block schedule. This format is popular because you can get a quick view of the week's activities on a single sheet of paper. The standard block schedule does not suit all students. Some prefer to use a listing of activities on daily sheets or in a bound planner, a format that allows the student to write more about upcoming activities.

When you complete a weekly schedule, begin by listing those activities that you consider a fixed commitment in your day, that is, activities that must occur at a set time, such as classes and labs, meetings, appointments, work, and so on. Next, consider those activities that you have more flexibility with scheduling, such as meals and sleep. Especially note study and leisure time, since typically these are at odds with one another. However, they do not have to be; you can use your study time and leisure time to complement one another as you go about your daily routine.

Daily Schedule

If you checked items 3, 5, 7, 8, 9, or 11 on the time management checklist, you will benefit from using a daily schedule. Of the three types of schedules, a daily schedule tends to be the most specific. This schedule simply consists of activities that need to be accomplished during a day. This list of daily events and reminders can be part of a weekly schedule, or it can be on a separate sheet of paper or note pad. Students often prioritize a day's activities according to importance or time frame. By referring to a daily schedule, you remember the multitude of details that occur throughout a day. As with the other schedules, keep this daily schedule handy for frequent referral.

Reflection Point 1

Think about the type of schedule you presently use:

What items on the time management checklist do you regularly schedule on a regular basis?

_____

_____

_____

So what can you do to improve how you manage your time?

_____

_____

_____

Now what type of time management schedule might work best for you?

_____

_____

_____

Changing Your Study Environment

You have made some choices about *when* to study; now you are going to evaluate *where* you study. Putting the time into studying is not enough if you are not in an environment that is conducive to working. Use the assessment in Exhibit 8.2 to begin to examine the places you currently use for study.

In the first column, indicate where you study most often; be specific, such as "second floor carrels in library," or "desk in residence hall room." In the second column, indicate the place you use second most often for studying. For each place answer the twelve observation items by checking "Usually," "Sometimes," or "Rarely."

Exhibit 8.2. Study Environment Assessment.

Observation

	#1 place _____			#2 place _____		
	Usually	Sometimes	Rarely	Usually	Sometimes	Rarely
1.	___	___	___	___	___	___
2.	___	___	___	___	___	___
3.	___	___	___	___	___	___
4.	___	___	___	___	___	___
5.	___	___	___	___	___	___
6.	___	___	___	___	___	___
7.	___	___	___	___	___	___
8.	___	___	___	___	___	___
9.	___	___	___	___	___	___
10.	___	___	___	___	___	___
11.	___	___	___	___	___	___
12.	___	___	___	___	___	___
TOTAL:	___	___	___	___	___	___

The higher the total score for each place, the fewer the distractions, and, therefore, the better that place is for study. Ideally, the places students use most often (#1 place) are the places with the higher scores.

Be aware of what distracts you when you are studying. It helps to think of distractions in terms of external and internal types. *External distractions* are things from an outside source that can divert your attention from concentrated study, such as loud noises or friends stopping by. *Internal distractions* are those distractions that originate from within yourself, such as feelings of being tired, hungry, bored, or apathetic.

Exhibit 8.2. Study Environment Assessment. *(continued)*

Observations

1. I fall asleep when I study here.
2. I think about things unrelated to schoolwork when I study here.
3. I think about breaks when I study here.
4. I get bored easily here.
5. I tend to look around the room or out a window when I study here.
6. I do other tasks besides studying here.
7. I often hear outside noise or music here.
8. My friends stop by while I am here.
9. I talk to others here.
10. I have easy access to a telephone here.
11. I hear other people talking here.
12. I turn on the television when I study here.

Scoring: For each study place, give yourself 0 points for each *Usually*, 1 point for each *Sometimes*, and 2 points for each *Rarely*.

Total Score:	*Rating:*
20–24	An excellent study place!
12–19	A fair study place, but you should reduce distractions or move elsewhere if you can.
0–11	A poor study place. Find another location!

Reflection Point 2

Think about your study environment:

What are the external distractions and internal distractions on your list?

_____

_____

_____

So what are more difficult to change: external or internal distractions? Why?

_____

_____

_____

Now what can you do to reduce or eliminate your study distractions?

_____

_____

_____

Listening Effectively

Listening is an important skill for success in many college courses. You have probably been in a course where you have been expected to listen to a professor talk for an hour or more and then be able to remember what is important within that presentation. Taking notes while you listen can enhance your understanding of the material covered in class.

Before a Lecture

What type of preparation do you do before class? Preparation can vary according to the type of class and type of subject. However, doing some type of work before a lecture helps students prepare themselves to understand the material and to participate in class.

Tips for Preparation for a Lecture Class

1. Read and study the accompanying text material beforehand. This is helpful if the lecture is going to follow the text material, *and* you understand the material better from the text than from the lecture.

2. Preview or skim the text material beforehand. This technique is helpful if the lecture is going to follow the text material, *and* you understand your professor's lecture better than the text. After the lecture, read, study, and mark the text more thoroughly.

3. Review the notes from the previous lecture. This is especially useful if your professor did not finish a topic or if a lesson is connected to the previous lecture. Spend ten minutes before class skimming over your notes from the last lecture, refreshing your memory about key ideas and organizational patterns.

4. Go over written assignments, such as math problems, workbook pages, or essays. Since your professor will probably dwell on what you did for homework, take several minutes before class to refresh yourself on the problems and topics at hand.

During a Lecture

The purpose of note taking during a lecture is to help you understand what is being presented as well as to give you something to refer to when studying the material. The four key words to remember are *clarity, speed, conciseness,* and *completeness.*

Tips for Taking Effective Notes

1. Clarity—write the idea clearly enough for you to read and understand but do not become unduly concerned about neatness.

2. Speed—write the idea quickly.

3. Conciseness—use as few words as possible to get the idea across.

4. Completeness—represent the whole idea accurately in your notes.

Be generous with your use of paper. To have clear, understandable notes, use space to your advantage. Use space to separate ideas, to indicate material that needs to be filled in later, and to generally aid in organizing lecture information. Avoid crowding too many ideas on a single sheet.

Most students want to write their notes as quickly as possible. Abbreviations and symbols can help you condense the amount of words needed to get the ideas across. Abbreviations and symbols fall into two main categories: general abbreviations and symbols that can be carried over from class to class, and those abbreviations and symbols that are particular to one subject area. For example, the abbreviations "frnt/bck," "w/o," "defi," and "cont'd" and symbols such as "&," "<," "#," and "@" are universal from one subject to another. On the other hand, "psych," "econ," "calc," and "CO_2" are particular to subjects you may be taking.

After a Lecture

An effective, efficient system of study depends upon the integration of classroom activity with study activity. An important strategy is examining lecture material soon after class, *while it is still fresh in your mind.*

Tips for Lecture Review

---

1. Go over your notes as soon as possible, taking the following steps whenever they seem appropriate:

   Highlighting key words or phrases

   Summarizing important ideas in the margins or back of the notepaper

   Filling in blanks by referring to your textbook or asking your professor for additional explanations

   Identifying areas that you are unsure about

   Coordinating lecture material with text or workbook material

   Formulating potential test questions

2. Go over your notes again on a weekly basis to consolidate the information from class to class. This type of review will not only refresh your memory about information from previous classes, it will also provide you with an overview of important ideas being presented. Steps include the following:

Flip through the pages of your notebook, focusing on those key ideas you have highlighted or jotted in the margins from lecture to lecture.

As you read each page, recite the information that you want to remember.

Recitation is a simple yet effective technique to aid recall (Shepherd, 1992). If you not only look at the information but also *say* it and *hear* it, you will be more likely to remember it.

The time you invest for review is learning time, which means that you will *know* the material when the test rolls around. This also means less need for cramming and long study hours before an exam.

Exercise 2: The Lecture

What are recommended strategies before, during, and after a lecture that promote active listening? What can you do to promote these active listening and note-taking strategies in your classes?

_____

_____

_____

_____

Reading Effectively

Effective reading does require effort; it is an active process that involves thinking and discovery. As with effective listening skills, effective reading skills depend upon your being *selective* about what you are reading. You must constantly ask yourself: What do I really have to know?

On Exhibit 8.3, check all the behaviors or attitudes that describe you and your academic reading. In this section you will read about strategies that refer to each of the twelve items in this assessment.

Getting an Overview: Prereading

What did you do the first time you entered the dining hall at your college or university? Did you pause for a few seconds to survey the situation and get your bearings? To see where the cafeteria line began? Find the trays? The salad bar? The desserts? Any familiar faces? A good place to sit? If you're like most people, you stopped for a quick overview—as you would before proceeding into any new environment.

Exhibit 8.3. Reading Assessment.

☐ 1. I dislike long reading assignments.

☐ 2. I have problems identifying the main ideas when I read.

☐ 3. I have problems concentrating when I read.

☐ 4. I avoid writing in textbooks.

☐ 5. I know text details for at least one subject I have this term.

☐ 6. I often find reading to be boring.

☐ 7. I procrastinate when it comes to reading assignments.

☐ 8. I have problems remembering what I read.

☐ 9. I am a *visual* learner—that is, I remember best when I see ideas in print.

☐ 10. I am an *auditory* learner—that is, I remember best when I hear ideas.

☐ 11. I have a short attention span when it comes to reading a textbook.

☐ 12. I tend to highlight a lot when I read.

It is useful to apply the same approach to reading a new textbook. This overview helps one to become more adept at coping with unfamiliar situations in print. Items 3, 6, 8, and 11 on the reading assessment examine your prereading skills. Getting a feel for what you are going to encounter in the textbook, chapter, or article will give you a head start. Providing yourself with an overview of the material will better equip you to deal with the ideas to be presented within the text. This stage is termed *prereading* because it consists of quick steps you do before you actually begin reading the new material.

Previewing the Textbook

What are the parts of a textbook that you can glance at to get yourself familiar with the content? Note the preface, introduction, copyright date, table of contents, index, appendixes, and answer keys. You need only do this step once a semester when you have just gotten the text and before you begin reading the first chapter.

Previewing the Chapter

You are now ready to get an overview of the chapter you are going to read. In this step you will be *anticipating* what it is that you will be reading about. Previewing a chapter prepares you by giving you background on the material you are about to read. You are cutting down on any surprises you are likely to encounter with new material, such as subject matter, length, difficulty level, and anticipated reading time.

Purpose

An additional facet of the prereading stage is to identify your purpose for reading the chapter. Why are you reading this? Is it to gain more knowledge about the topic or to become a well-read individual? Or is it because the chapter was assigned or because you want to do well on the upcoming test? Identifying your purpose for reading leads you to identify how much and what type of information you need to know. For peak reading efficiency be clear as to why you are reading and how much information you need to retain.

A System of Reading and Studying

The effective reader is able to integrate the reading process with the studying process. You should be reading, checking your understanding, and setting up a method for review (that is, studying) at the same time. Items 1, 3, 7, 8, and 11 on the reading assessment consider your present methods for reading and study.

An important step in tackling text material is to *break up your reading*. It is not feasible to expect yourself to read a thirty-page chapter at one fell swoop and really understand and remember the important material for an exam. After you have read an entire chapter it is almost too late to ask yourself if you understand the material. If you do not understand, the only recourse is to go back over the entire chapter, certainly an inefficient means of comprehending. Instead, it is beneficial to read a *section* at a time, stop, and then ask yourself if you understand what you just read.

If you aren't able to paraphrase the important ideas in the section, you'll need to read the material again.

If you are able to understand the chapter section, now is the time to *write down important ideas* so as to create a study guide for yourself. By developing a study guide, you are reinforcing immediate understanding and creating a guide for future recall.

Choosing a Study Guide

You can choose from several types of study guides depending upon the type of material you are reading, how much information you need to know, and what technique you feel most comfortable using.

Developing Questions

If you develop questions for yourself, you usually have an easier time anticipating what it is that you need to know from the text material. Items 2, 3, 4, 6, 8, 11, and 12 on the reading assessment measure this concept. Using each section heading or subheading as a basis for forming a question is the simplest way to begin this type of study guide—the headings serve as topic titles for each section of text and should key into the material to be presented. Turn the heading into a question that will guide you toward identifying the main idea. Then write down an answer to the question after reading the section (Pauk, 1997).

Exercise 3: Question Priorities

Consider the six question words in the upcoming list. What is the difference between the words listed in column one versus the words listed in column two?

What	When
Why	Who
How	Where

The words in column one will guide you toward identifying the main ideas of a section, whereas the words in column two guide you toward details. Avoid the question words in column two unless they are used in conjunction with the words in column one. In other words, if you need to know specific details as well as main ideas, you can make a question using *when, who,* or *where* as a supplement to the open-ended question using *what, why,* or *how.*

The technique in Exercise 3 is especially helpful in these three situations:

- If you have a lot of pages to read. If your reading is piling up and you are feeling overwhelmed by the quantity of pages, this technique can get you through the material at a relatively quick pace.

- If you have difficulty identifying the main idea of a section. Answering the open-ended questions should point you toward the important ideas.

- If you have problems concentrating on your reading.

By turning reading into a process of discovering answers to questions, you become a more active learner and, as a result, tend to improve your concentration.

Taking Separate Notes—Mapping and Study Cards

Separate notes are especially helpful when you need to know not only main ideas, but also many supporting ideas and details in your reading. In addition, if you do not want to or are unable to write in your book, you must make a study guide by creating separate notes. *Mapping* is a note-taking technique by which you develop a visual picture of the words in print (Hanf, 1971). If you checked items 2, 4, 5, 8, 9, or 12 on the reading assessment, you may benefit from mapping. Other terms used to describe a similar process include *idea chunking, webbing, flowcharting, mind mapping,* and *networking.* Mapping provides an excellent means for summarizing written material. The general format for mapping looks like this:

Topic

Main idea   **Main idea**

Supporting   Supporting   Supporting   Supporting
idea   idea   idea   idea

Detail   Detail

Here is an example of a passage that will benefit from being mapped:

> Many physiological differences between the sexes have been found. These differences include the following: females tend to be more sensitive to sounds, more proficient at fine motor performance, and more attentive to social cues. On the other hand, males have a visual and spatial superiority. These differences affect how each sex processes information.

And here is the corresponding map:

physiological differences affecting learning

females	males
sensitive to sounds	visually superior
fine motor performance	spatially superior
attentive to social cues	

Study cards are developed by students to capture main ideas, definitions, and other important information that must be learned and retained in memory. If you checked items 1, 4, 5, 6, 8, 9, 10, 11, or 12 on the reading assessment you may benefit from the use of study cards. Study cards have several advantages:

- Cards help students be selective, especially with longer readings. Students who are adept at developing study cards can readily pull out topics and supporting details as they read through a text. Given the limited space on cards, students must be concise when writing down information.

- Cards are good for drill work, especially for terminology and details. A cautionary note: Students who use study cards tend to rely on memorizing the information. Putting information in your own words and adding examples should help you increase understanding and not just recall. If you are required to synthesize or apply text information, your study cards should reflect this requirement, or you should develop an alternative study guide.

- Study cards can provide both auditory and visual reinforcement of information. Cards lend themselves to study games such as classmates' quizzing each other or teaching one another, or students' seeing and saying the information aloud to themselves, or peer groups' writing potential test questions and answers for one another. Because of their versatility, study cards are helpful for students with short attention spans when reading and studying.

Improving Your Reading Concentration

Items 3, 6, 7, and 11 on the reading assessment ask questions related to how well you concentrate when you read. The following techniques help you improve your reading concentration. If you find your reading boring or tedious, try these:

Check Marks

Put a check mark on the margin of the page or on a separate sheet of paper every time you notice that your mind wanders. This self-awareness of when and how often your mind wanders will help you improve your concentration. You will notice a steady decrease in check marks and improved concentration as you use this technique (Pauk, 1997).

Kitchen Timer

Begin by asking yourself how many minutes you can read without losing your concentration: ten minutes? fifteen minutes? Set a kitchen timer to that amount of time; when the timer goes off take a short break. Then set the timer and begin again. Knowing that you have a set amount of time to read before taking a break will help you sharpen your concentration. Students who use this technique often report that they gradually lengthen the amount of time that they can read attentively.

Worry Sheet

If your reading concentration is faltering because of personal problems, try this method. On a sheet of paper make three columns:

WHAT I'm Worried About: **HOW I'll Tackle It:**   **WHEN I'll Tackle It:**

Writing down a specific plan of action such as this will help unburden your mind and, as a result, improve your concentration for the immediate task of reading (Pauk, 1997).

Exercise 4: Textbook Reading

What are recommended strategies that lead to effective and efficient textbook reading? What can you do to promote these active reading and studying strategies in your courses?

_____

_____

_____

_____

_____

Preparing for Exams

What do you do to prepare for a major test? Three interrelated study areas are linked to test preparation: managing study time, reviewing class material, and practicing for the test.

Managing Study Time

All too often students end up cramming the night before a test. How about you? When do you typically begin to study for the test?

For a major test, it's a good idea to begin studying five to seven days before the exam. This assumes that you have kept up with your study guides for your reading and have regularly reviewed your lecture notes. Add chunks of extra study time during the week to review material needed for the exam. Even if you are not in the habit of using a weekly schedule, now is the time to develop one, especially if you have two or more tests falling within a few days of each other. If you plan ahead and write down when you intend to study, you are more apt to follow through with the time commitments.

Reviewing Class Material

First, you will want to know as much as possible about the test so as to efficiently direct your studying for the week before the test. "What do I really need to know for this test?" is a question you should ask yourself before you begin any intensive studying. You want to be as clear as possible about the material the test will cover, where the emphasis will be placed (text or lecture material), how long the test will be, what type of questions will be on the test, and if there are any time constraints. Of course, the foremost avenue for finding out about the test is your instructor. If your instructor does not volunteer this information, *ask*.

During this extra time in the week preceding an exam, you will want to be as selective as possible and concentrate on what is important to know for the test.

Tips for Boiling Down Information for a Test

1. Outline or list key ideas from lectures, earlier tests, and other sources.
2. Highlight key ideas in your notes and study guides.
3. Organize information within categories as much as possible.
4. Devise note cards with important terms or ideas.
5. Develop a map or chart to provide a visual overview of material.
6. Summarize information in your own words, within a few paragraphs.

These methods are not only effective for review of course material, they also provide a means to refresh you the day or two before an exam. It is during this time period—twenty-four to forty-eight hours preceding the exam—that, by reciting and reflecting on the information over and over again, you can reinforce the material so that it is stamped into your memory, ready to be retrieved and used for the exam!

Practicing for the Test

Practice tests can be an excellent method of studying for an upcoming exam because they enable the student to review and reinforce subject content and also anticipate and practice specific types of questions on the test.

Ask your instructor if there are samples of earlier tests that you can look at as you study. Often instructors keep former tests on file or on reserve in the library. In addition, use the questions at the end of a chapter or accompanying workbook or study guide. Making up your own test questions can be another effective study method. Not only does this allow you to go over the subject matter and select important ideas, it also gives you a chance to formulate questions. This is a recommended strategy for group study.

Reflection Point 3

Think about test preparation:

What are recommended methods for preparing for a test?

_____

_____

_____

So what methods do you make use of?

_____

_____

_____

Now what can you do before to be fully prepared for upcoming tests and exams?

_____

_____

_____

Summary

In your role as peer educator others will view you as an accomplished student, one who has developed a personal study system that is a model for others. In this chapter you assessed and evaluated your own study techniques in the areas of time management and study environment, lecture listening and note taking, textbook reading, and test preparation. Armed with this information, you are now better prepared to recommend and demonstrate college-level study strategies to your peers, especially those struggling with the academic demands of college. You are ready to guide fellow students in the development of their own system of study; as a result, you will feel the satisfaction that comes from playing a key role in other students' academic success.

Chapter Eight: Summary Questions

1. In your own words, define "system of study."

   _____

   _____

   _____

   _____

2. What is the relationship between one's system of study and active learning?

   _____

   _____

   _____

   _____

3. Describe three behaviors that promote active learning for each of these study areas: time management, study environment, lecture listening, lecture note taking, textbook reading, and test preparation.

   _____

   _____

   _____

   _____

9

Using Campus Resources and Referral Techniques

Learning Objectives

After completing this chapter the peer educators will be able to

1. List available campus and community resources.

2. Assess the appropriateness of campus and community resources for use by students.

3. Take advantage of consultation with available professional staff and other knowledgeable sources of information when making informed decisions for assisting students.

4. Refer students to appropriate campus and community resources.

5. Offer post-referral follow-up and support.

A recent newspaper article headlined the hypothetical consumer notice, "Warning: attending college can be dangerous to your health." The article referred to a common theme in news stories concerning today's generation of college students, who are facing a level of complexity and change in their lives that was unknown to their predecessors even a few years ago. Students today have an escalating number of choices they must make about their careers and personal life. They must adapt rapidly to changes in technology that make last year's inventions quickly obsolete.

Their world has shrunk to a figurative backyard of international opportunity in which Internet communication, multinational businesses, and intercultural exchanges are a daily reality. At the same time, the rules and norms of society are in more flux than ever before with a myriad of options for social contact and intimacy—the important areas where individuals receive support and security in their lives. Whereas the more traditional family and societal standards of a few years ago set down a template of expectations for former generations to follow, the new generation has a proliferation of life options and ultimately more confusion as to what are the most important and valuable standards to assist their decision process. Many experts observing this phenomenon have noted the increased levels of stress, feelings of alienation, and survival living—which emphasizes immediate gratification instead of long-term direction (Newton, 1998).

Students, more than ever before, need to make use of resources to assist in managing the decisions, stresses, and information overload of the present world. And, as Ian Birky, a director of counseling, points out, "Students often are trying to go it alone, giving rise to more stress and anxiety than they can handle, when they need to reach out to someone else to talk about how they are feeling and managing the exhaustive pressure in their drive to succeed . . . many do not know how to seek out this help!" (Cited in Vigoda, 1998, p. 1.)

A very important role for the peer educator is to assist students as they seek, find, and contact necessary resources outside their daily routine. Students serving in helping roles must have a firm grasp of available campus and community resources and know their appropriate uses. In addition to a knowledge of resources, it is important that the peer educator learn how to direct students to these resources effectively.

Campus and Community Resources

When any student strives to achieve a goal, whether it is academic success, overcoming a personal obstacle, or achieving a new skill, the effort will almost certainly entail the use of special resources. Every campus has in place an array of people and services with primary responsibility for providing this sort of assistance. Student affairs offices, various academic services, faculty members, community services, and even private businesses are potential sources for information and aid. Most of these forms of assistance will involve human resources, but there are also many physical facilities and technological resources. For example, Web pages, media kiosks, or other facilities that make use of electronic interactive media can provide information formerly available only from face-to-face interviews or library searches. Help telephone lines and 800 or 888 connections are additional sources. Knowing where to go for what becomes a crucial bit of information for effective peer helping.

Many students are not familiar with their campus and community resources, and thus are unable to take advantage of them. Another problem students face when contemplating the use of campus resources is the misinformation and rumors that sometimes circulate about an office, service, or resource. Both lack of information and misinformation can quickly block use of a resource that could be a valuable asset in personal goal accomplishment.

At times, students may feel reluctant and even embarrassed to admit needing help. Even asking a question of a faculty member after class may be difficult for fear of appearing stupid. Therefore, peer educators can play a significant role in providing objective and reassuring information about the resources available. In your role you may be called upon to share information about the existence of a resource or about its adequacy and quality, sometimes dispelling myths that might otherwise discourage students from taking advantage of available services.

It is also noteworthy that peer educators can often provide evaluative feedback to campus and community resources regarding the students' perception of the services in question. This information gives the agency, program, or department the opportunity to clarify its role, improve publicity, and even improve the quality of its services and interaction with students.

Students will often hang back and avail themselves of support services and resource opportunities only when a situation has reached critical proportions. Peer educators can provide an important and advantageous service by getting a student to sources of assistance before the crisis breaks, when prevention and early intervention are possible. Ideally, campus resources are best used to help students achieve their personal and academic goals before those goals have been threatened by a developing problem.

When to Refer

Frequently, the beginning peer educator finds it difficult to determine when to refer a student to another resource. It is natural to want to help—that's what draws people into the peer educator role—but watch out if you find yourself feeling pressured to relieve and resolve the concern of the person requesting and needing assistance. This pressure can lead to a tendency to give quick advice, offering a solution by providing a suggestion out of your own repertoire of answers or immediately directing the student to another resource that seems likely to hold the solution. Often, your own solution may not be the answer to someone else's concerns, and a quick referral may feel like a brush-off or the beginning of a runaround. The following guidelines (adapted from Ender, Saunders-McCaffrey, and Miller, 1979) will help you make adequate and welcome referrals.

Listen Carefully

The first and often the most important step is to listen carefully and clearly so as to understand what the individual needs in the way of assistance. Look back to Chapter Four for a discussion of the process of becoming an effective communicator. And remember, as a peer, you will probably be perceived as an approachable, friendly source to ask for assistance. Your support, encouragement, and guidance may be sufficient to help an individual figure out what to do, but there will be times when the student's concern is beyond your knowledge, greater than you wish to handle, or otherwise in need of professional attention. This is the point when you consider referral.

Know Your Limits

The second important item to address regarding referrals is to know your own limits for giving assistance. As a general rule, when in doubt, refer the student to a more qualified resource. Trying to help a student with a serious problem when you possess only minimal skill and experience in that area may do more harm than good. Take, for example, the peer educator who, with little knowledge about the world of work, attempts to assist a student in clarifying a career decision. Such a student is apt to believe that the help received is the help needed in this area, and may therefore be reluctant to seek additional assistance from a more qualified source. The student may waste valuable time following a course of action that does not fit their real needs, such as majoring in a field that proves to be without long-term interest to them, and this may eventually lead to frustration with the process.

Seek Consultation

Sometimes there may be an intermediate step between understanding a student's needs and setting up a referral. This step is for the helper to seek a consultation with a knowledgeable resource person to find out about options for the student being helped. The student being assisted would first be informed that you, as a peer educator, would like to consult with another source that can give suggestions or input as to the next step in assistance. Using the example of the career issue previously mentioned, you could say, "I would like to talk to a counselor at the Career Counseling Office and get their suggestions as to activities that might be helpful for the questions you are having. Would you mind if I call them and get back to you with their suggestions?" By clarifying what you are seeking from a consultation and getting the student's consent, you are enabling the student to be informed and in control of this process. Sometimes such a consultation can be made by phone with the student present, in other cases it may be preferable for the peer educator to meet with a resource then get back to the student in a timely way. When seeking consultative assistance, it is important to have clear and complete information about the needs of the student you are representing.

While consultation may take place through a person with expertise in an area of assistance, peer educators will also routinely seek consultation from the person who serves as the supervisor. It is important to regularly review the processes you are using as a helper and get feedback as to the appropriateness of your interventions and referrals.

How to Refer

When you refer someone to another resource, you want the referral to be seen as welcome assistance and not some sort of brush-off. The following guidelines (adapted from Ender, Saunders-McCaffrey, and Miller, 1979) will help you accomplish effective referrals.

Be Honest

Be direct and straightforward in your recommendation. Explain in a clear and open manner why you feel it is desirable or necessary to make a referral.

Become Knowledgeable

Explain fully the services that can be obtained from the resource agency or person you are recommending. Provide confirming data about how the referral source can be useful and describe the source's qualifications or capabilities. This information can be reassuring to the student so that they will receive the help they need. It is preferable to avoid making a "shot in the dark" referral or providing information that might turn into a runaround because you do not know for sure that the agency has the assistance that matches the student's need. Check it out!

Demonstrate Respect

Allow the student to assume responsibility and control in making a contact or appointment. Student initiation and follow-up enhance commitment and promote a sense of autonomy in taking charge of the situation.

Personalize the Referral Process

It can be useful to give the student the name of a particular person or persons who can be a direct contact at the resource organization. This will personalize and make the experience seem less intimidating. Be careful about this sort of referral, though. It may be best to not provide the name of anyone who may be hard to contact or may seem less available than a general referral.

Role-Play or Practice

Assist the student in formulating questions to ask or approaches to take during an initial contact session. Some rehearsal or preparation can be reassuring.

Carefully Assess the Need

In some cases you may find a student resists or denies the need to go to a professional resource. You have several choices when you meet such resistance. You can accept the individual's decision to not take advantage of the referral. If you believe the individual simply needs more encouragement, you can provide more explicit reasons why you believe it is important for them to go. If the problem is uneasiness about approaching an office, you could consider more direct assistance such as offering to go with them to make an initial contact. Finally, if you believe there is the potential of danger to self or others, such as reference to a suicidal threat, you should go to the professional resource on your campus on your own so as to get consultation and assistance to aid that individual.

Follow Up

Encourage the student to get back in touch with you after visiting the recommended resource. In some cases, it would be appropriate to make the contact yourself if you don't hear back from the student in a reasonable time. This shows your concern and interest and provides continuity of the helping relationship. Also, this follow-up contact with the student provides additional incentive for the student to make contact with the referral source.

Reflection Point 1

Think of a time when you personally have needed to find out about a campus resource or needed information:

What obstacles or difficulties did you encounter in trying to get your situation resolved?

_____

_____

_____

So what was the personal impact on you when dealing with these obstacles? Imagine someone else going through a similar situation to what you experienced.

_____

_____

_____

_____

Now what could you do to reduce the hassles and obstacles in getting what was needed?

_____

_____

_____

_____

Chat Rooms and Other Online Resources

In today's world, more and more students gain immediate access to other individuals, sometimes so-called experts, by way of e-mail, the Internet, and numerous self-help networks. Many students spend hours in Internet chat rooms, trying to meet a significant person through a media dating exchange, or joining a network of people who have similar interests, and become outlets for information and sometimes support. Although this can be an immediate source of contact at almost any time of day on almost any subject, students need to be very aware of the many potential problems associated with this resource.

First, using interactive computer and other media contact provides very little control over the authenticity of individual responses or of the message and information being communicated. Additionally, revealing personal information has little assurance of privacy or confidentiality, and may even be used in ways that are fraudulent or harassing. There are certainly occasions in which valid information and support can be gained from the Internet and similar resources, however, the "buyer should always beware" of possible misleading information or deceits. Do not assume that a chat room can replace direct contact in face-to-face situations with a person or office of established reputation. Technology has produced an extensive resource for gaining information and developing rapid and expansive communication systems, but face-to-face contact is still the most direct and personal way to respond to individual needs and circumstances.

Guidelines for Learning About Campus and Community Resources

Before you tell someone to try a resource or service, you should make sure you know what it does best and how to take advantage of it. It is your responsibility to avoid spreading misinformation and dropping students into a frustrating runaround.

Tips for Evaluating Resources

The following tips (adapted from Ender, Saunders-McCaffrey, and Miller, 1979) will be helpful as you evaluate referral resources.

1. Visit the service. Meet with staff members of the resources most frequently used by the students with whom you work. This process is time-consuming but provides many important benefits. It is easier to make an effective and reassuring referral if you know something about the beliefs and attributes of the persons at a particular office, as well as having a knowledge of the services provided.

2. Tour the facility. Ask for a tour of facilities and material resources such as library, media collection, or computer lab. Familiarity with the physical facilities will also enable you to refer a student to the most appropriate resource available. Ask to be on any mailing list the office has for announcing special events or programs. Get a copy of any descriptive brochure—with extras to hand out if they're readily available.

3. Understand the agency's referral process. Ask specific questions regarding referral procedures, activities of the office, office hours, and even the philosophy or attitudes of the staff toward providing service. Discover the process a student goes through when seeking assistance, such as filling out forms and scheduling appointments. Find out if the agency has a policy regarding confidentiality.

4. Check out willingness to serve as consultants. Explore the possibilities of using agency resource persons as consultants for helping you work with students. For example, if you were working with a student who has experienced a personal crisis, it would be very useful to know how to access a counseling psychologist or similar personal counselor to find out about dealing with crisis and referral.

Reflection Point 2

Think about your own work with other students and the limits of your skills:

What benefits can peer educators derive from having knowledge of campus and community resources?

_____

_____

_____

_____

So what criteria does one use when deciding if a referral is an appropriate strategy? Looking at the reverse standard, when would it be inappropriate to use referral?

_____

_____

_____

_____

Now what competencies and knowledge must you, the peer educator, possess to be an effective referral agent?

_____

_____

_____

Summary

Knowledge of available campus and community resources and of appropriate ways to make a referral will be an effective tool for a peer educator to use in work with students. The more you know about the purpose and function of various offices, the more effective you will be in helping students develop plans, solve problems, and achieve their goals.

There are numerous services, facilities, and sources of information at your disposal as you work with other students. Timely, appropriate referrals to these services will become a significant aspect of your work. Take time to get to know and understand the substantial benefits these resources offer to students. Network with others who share your goal of assisting students as they maximize their college experience.

Chapter Nine: Summary Questions

1. List two possible campus or community resources for each of the following student concerns: dating problems, parental problems, roommate problems, overweight, financial problems, sexual harassment, difficulty with study, test anxiety, legal problems, sexually transmitted disease, conflict with a faculty member, and lack of social life.

_____

_____

_____

_____

_____

_____

_____

_____

_____

_____

_____

2. List four or more reasons why a referral may be an important intervention for a peer helper to offer.

_____

_____

_____

_____

_____

3. What are some general guidelines to follow when using another
service or person in a consulting capacity?

_____

_____

_____

_____

4. What are several guidelines to follow when making an effective
referral?

_____

_____

_____

_____

_____

10

Ethics and Strategies for Good Practice

Learning Objectives

After completing this chapter the peer educators will be able to

1. Understand the ethics of working with other students.

2. Describe strategies for good practice in the peer educator's role.

———————

A s a peer educator, you are entering into a branch of the helping professions. In nearly all professions, individuals are subject to standards for practice and a code of conduct. These lists of ethical behaviors help spell out the appropriate conduct for fulfilling the profession's roles and responsibilities when providing a service to others. Typically, these rules are based upon a consensus of practicing professionals. For example, U.S. physicians adhere to a set of standards developed by their professional membership group, the American Medical Association. As a peer educator you will not be identified as a professional, but you are still responsible for maintaining good practice in the delivery of acceptable services. This final chapter suggests guidelines and principles that would be a good standard for you to implement in your own work.

Standard of Ethical Practice for Peer Educators

It is extremely important for you as a peer educator to understand and practice ethical behavior as you work with other students. The first step is to identify and understand what a code of ethics might include for peer educators. This awareness can be accomplished by having a clear written statement that outlines standards of conduct, by reviewing and discussing this in training, and by working under the supervision of an adviser or professional mentor. We recommend that the content of an ethical statement consider at least the following points:

- Peer educators will have knowledge and act consistently with any professional standards that are appropriate to the agency in which they are employed.

- Peer educators will respect the autonomy and individual dignity of the students they serve.

- Peer educators will avoid acting beyond the scope of service for which they were selected and trained, and not attempt to offer professional services requiring more extensive qualifications and training.

- Peer educators will maintain the right to privacy and confidentiality of the students for whom they serve.

- Peer educators will act in their practice for the benefit and welfare of students, being careful to avoid issues in which conflict of interest, bias, or dual relationship could jeopardize this helping stance.

Principles to Enhance the Quality of Peer Practice

The ethical statements listed in the preceding section will serve to assist you, your institution, and outside agencies as all strive to promote high-quality, ethical services for students. These statements will also assist you as you work to implement your role in a competent manner. On a daily basis you will be confronted with issues that have ethical implications. Although there is no blueprint as to how to approach the multitude of unique circumstances you will confront, we believe there are some principles for good practice that you can use as criteria for future decision making. These strategies can be sorted in regard to your skill level as determined by training, your relationship with your supervisor, your relationship with the students seeking your services, and your relationship with the university and community at large.

Skills as Determined by Training

By far, your level of helping skills—determined by the training program designed to develop your ability to work with others—is the criterion that you should apply when making most decisions as you work with others.

PRINCIPLE 1: Respond within the limits of your training and skill.

When you receive requests for information, assistance, or support that require skills beyond your training, expertise, or jurisdiction you must know your personal limits and not exceed the boundaries of your knowledge and skills by making suggestions or implying knowledge that may be lacking. An appropriate response in these situations is to state clearly that you do not have the expertise or information to help in the area. If possible you can briefly explain the reason or limits of your assistance without coming across as rejecting the student you are serving or withholding something you could provide if you chose. If you have knowledge of an appropriate referral source, that information should be shared and assistance offered in getting the person to the resource.

PRINCIPLE 2: Acknowledge your limits openly by saying that you do not know rather than pretending false expertise.

Even within the limits of your role, you will be asked questions whose answers you do not know. Do not play the role of expert. Saying, "I don't know" is much more helpful than faking it. When confronted with this situation, acknowledge your shortcomings and work with the person seeking help to find the right answer. This may involve consultation with other peer educators or your supervisor, or making calls around campus to discover the information needed. In many cases, problem solving on how to find solutions is even more helpful than having the answer for someone. As the adage says, "It is better to teach people to fish than to give them fish."

Relationship with Your Supervisor

Your supervisor is the most important contact you have in your role as a peer educator. Your supervisor will serve as your mentor, coach, employer, and guide in the area of helping others. This relationship is critical to your success.

PRINCIPLE 3: When in doubt—consult!

When you are confronted with a situation in which you are uncertain as to what to do or believe there may be some conflict or dilemma it is a critical moment to consult with your supervisor. Use this person's expertise—as a professional in your service area who shares some responsibility for your success, your supervisor can be your greatest resource. Many people are tempted to try and shield uncertainties from a supervisor in the belief that the supervisor will somehow think less of them for not having the answer. In reality, the moments you have questions or doubts are the most important times to get supervisory input.

PRINCIPLE 4: Maintain client privacy and confidentiality as long as privacy protects the person being helped.

Ideally, your relationship with students seeking your services is private and the helping agreement implies that you will not divulge personal data about them. This standard of conduct protects the privacy of the individual, and it also promotes a level of trust that makes self-disclosure of personal information possible.

But there are exceptions to the rule of confidentiality. First, if you are receiving supervision it is both necessary and helpful to individuals being served for you to discuss aspects of the case with the supervisor. It is very important that a full disclosure be made to your client that states that you are being supervised and that you share information with that specific individual so as to improve your own service skills. The client then has the prerogative to agree with that condition or request an alternative. Another very important exception to maintaining a private and confidential stance with a student is when you have received information that reveals a potential danger to self or others. In these instances, you should consult with your supervisor or a responsible party at your institution, such as the dean of students, and determine an appropriate method for intervention by a resource of the campus or community that can act to prevent harm.

These exceptions are where the information stops. You should never gossip or otherwise casually reveal information received about another person that you have learned as a result of working with a student.

Relationships with Students Seeking Your Assistance

As in all helping situations, the interaction between two people—the quality of the relationship—is probably the most important factor in the success and helpfulness that occurs. The way in which a student requesting assistance perceives you and your skill is critical to the success that you will achieve with your efforts.

PRINCIPLE 5: Show respect and dignity for other individuals.

Tolerance and acceptance of both the individual student and their circumstances are important prerequisites for any assistance. No student with whom you work should be made to feel that you are condescending to them while you are serving in your role as helper. All contact—and information from that contact—should be maintained with respect, privacy, and confidentiality. The exceptions to this rule are when the student agrees that sharing with others is appropriate or if the information learned puts the student or the community in danger. Again, treat these matters as described in Principle Four.

PRINCIPLE 6: Understand your own personal bias and avoid imposing this bias on others.

Peer educators should be careful to not impose their personal bias on other students, or to attempt to influence or prejudice the student's views or beliefs. This might include criticism of other individuals or authorities, disenchantment, or strong value judgments that ask the student to deal with personal agendas received from you as a peer educator. Everyone has personal opinions and biases, but they should be stated with personal ownership and without a sense of pressuring or convincing another to accept that opinion.

PRINCIPLE 7: Continue to deal appropriately when working with persons for whom you feel some aversion.

You may find that in your role as a peer educator that you will meet and be asked to work with other students for whom you may feel some antagonism, dislike, or other strong emotional reaction. In these cases one must consider why the aversion is being experienced and carefully assess whether these feelings will interfere with the role that you are to maintain. For example, you may feel irritated because the person acts a lot like someone you know who has hurt you in the past. In some instances, it may be best to admit the limitation and find a way that the individual can be served by another person. It is useful to consult your supervisor about ways to handle such personality difficulties.

PRINCIPLE 8: Act appropriately when working with persons for whom you feel attraction.

At times, you may meet students in your work for whom you feel interest or even attraction. You may even recognize that you would like to have this person as a friend, a date, or a companion outside the activities of the job. These types of relationships can compromise your helping role and may set up problems of dual relationships. Avoidance of these dilemmas should be carefully discussed in peer training, emphasizing power differentials and influence when involved in a helping role. You should consider, beforehand, how to avoid or deal with these dilemmas should they occur. And if an incident should occur, talk with your supervisor about it.

PRINCIPLE 9: Knowing and managing your emotional response while helping another is crucial to your own well-being and to your ability to help.

As you serve in your role, you may evoke emotionally charged reactions from students ranging from anger and irritation to grief and sorrow. Peer educators must be prepared to know how to handle and even control emotional reactions by learning to set limits, accept but not absorb emotional output, and channel reactions through referral to appropriate resources on campus. On some occasions, a student reaction will stimulate parallel feelings from a peer educator's own experience. In these cases a peer educator must know how to follow up and use personal resources of support to debrief from such encounters. Stress debriefing after crisis intervention is a common practice for disaster relief personnel and others who deal with emergency traumatic situations—there's no need to tough it out on your own, and it won't make you look any stronger or more competent if you try to do so.

Relationships with Your University Community and Beyond

As a peer educator working on a college campus, you work in a residential and community setting. It is important to note that you have obligations to this community both as a peer educator and as a community member.

PRINCIPLE 10: Take responsible action if you learn about illegal behavior.

In your role, you may hear a student report information that may have elements of behavior that is illegal or potentially unethical. In this instance, you may confront the behavior in a manner that points out the social norms and consequences in a manner that suggests that you are not the person to judge the behavior, but that there are clear social norms and laws that one must deal with in a community or society. In the case where the information shared with you has a clear and present danger to others in the community, this information should be shared with your supervisor to determine the appropriate course of action.

PRINCIPLE 11: Remember that as a peer educator you are a role model!

As pointed out in Chapter One, peer educators are student role models, both on campus and in the community. This means you are obligated to maintain a congruence between what you say to fellow students in your role and how you act in other facets of your life where you will be seen (or heard) by those with whom you have worked. For example, if you help others with problems in the area of time management but you are the one who is always late to meetings, or if you are giving presentations on responsible drinking yet get picked up for a DUI, much of your credibility as a peer educator is quickly and decidedly undermined.

PRINCIPLE 12: Maintain integrity and do not promote hearsay in commenting on professional relationships with others.

In your role, students will ask for your opinion in regard to the quality of other professionals. This is especially true in reference to faculty on your campus and the type of classroom experience they offer. We believe you should refrain from giving negative opinions or at least limit any potentially critical comment to objective facts about a campus professional or agency. Everyone experiences other people differently. What may have been a poor experience for you could be quite excellent for others.

Exercise 1: Real-Life Ethics

Place yourself in the following situations:

You are talking with a student who describes having taken part in a felony.

You notice a student in a class in which you are a discussion leader with whom you have had an unresolved conflict over the past year.

You are very attracted to a person you have tutored in the past couple of weeks, and you are thinking about talking with a roommate about the possibility of dating this person.

What are the implications for ethical conduct in each case? Describe your options for handling each of these situations.

_____

_____

_____

_____

_____

_____

Exercise 2: Quality Assurance

The following Pledge for Quality Service was written for a peer counseling office and posted for clientele to view when they entered the service area. Read the sample pledge and design a similar statement that is adapted to your peer educator role.

Pledge. Our goal is to provide a helpful, user-friendly service to students. Our staff will strive to meet the following standards for a high-quality practice:

1. Privacy and confidentiality
2. Timely service
3. Courteous and helpful reception
4. Clear and specific goals for individual outcomes
5. Explanation of any strategy or procedure recommended
6. Information concerning referral options
7. Supervision from professional staff
8. Training of all staff prior to assuming position and continued weekly
9. Sensitivity to cultural and lifestyle differences

If these standards are not being met to your satisfaction you have the right to make this concern or complaint known to the director and will receive a response within two days.

_____

_____

_____

_____

_____

_____

_____

_____

_____

_____

_____

_____

Conclusion

To wind up your work in this training experience, we encourage you to work in collaboration with your fellow trainees and your trainer to develop a mutually acceptable statement of ethics. This may entail a series of statements of good practice to guide your work or a more formal statement of ethical practice. In either case, it is important that you have specific guidelines to evaluate your work and make decisions on a day-to-day basis.

_____

Chapter Ten: Summary Questions

1. Why do peer educators need ethical statements to guide their day-to-day practice?

_____

_____

_____

_____

_____

2. Twelve principles for good practice were presented in this chapter. What are the five most important to your role as a peer educator?

_____

_____

_____

_____

_____

_____

Epilogue

We have written this book to help you attain the knowledge and skills important to your role as a peer educator. We have also designed it to help you learn about yourself. We hope that through your reading and the rest of your training experience you have gained an understanding of your potentials, your strengths, and your weaknesses as they affect your ability to assist others.

Perhaps, during this training experience, you discovered areas of personal challenge in which you can make improvements so as to be a better role model for other students. Perhaps you have acknowledged feeling uncomfortable interacting with people from different races or ethnic backgrounds. Perhaps you recognized a tendency to be an avid advice giver more than a listener when providing assistance, or realized that discomfort with working with people in groups has inhibited your participation level and effectiveness in that setting. It was our intent, as authors of the book, to create the potential for these types of personal insights as you completed activities such as reflection points, group exercises, and summary questions.

The concepts identified in this book are intended to have universal application; that is, they apply to you as well as to the students who seek your assistance. If you have personally gained information about yourself that has created uncertainty and possible dissonance, the probability is that you will make changes and find opportunities to grow in your own development. You may wish to follow the problem-solving process, assessing where you are and where you would like to be with a view to identifying strategies that will lead to the achievement of your own goals. For example, to be a more effective student role model you may now be working hard to be on time for classes and appointments. Or if you were hesitant to accept others different from yourself you may now be taking the initiative and the personal risk to meet and talk with others from different races or cultural backgrounds. It is important to acknowledge that as a helping person you must address the personal challenges in your own life if you are to demonstrate understanding for other students who wish to change their behavior and function in more successful ways. As a partner in understanding change you will know and appreciate the hard work, energy, and dedication it takes to alter long-standing behavior. The most effective peer educators know their strengths and weaknesses and actively pursue courses of action to improve their own functioning both as human beings and as helpers.

Although personal knowledge and growth is important, we do not want to underemphasize the need to learn, demonstrate, and practice helping skills. We have particularly noted the need to learn and master interpersonal communications, problem-solving techniques, assessment techniques, group leadership, and the process of making referrals, and to demonstrate methods such as effective study techniques.

Training as preparation for the helping role is not the end of skill development, it is more like a basic starting point. You will need to continue to learn and enhance your knowledge and skills. We urge you to become a part of a continuing process of development in which you reflect on your interactions with others and determine ways to improve your approach to any situation. There are a number of ways to continue to develop your skills. For example, use consultation and continued training with your supervisor through regular supervision and in-service activities. Seek out resources and expertise from other community and campus-based agencies such as the Counseling Center, which offer personal skill-building opportunities.

We believe you will benefit from the peer educator role in many positive and long-lasting ways. The skills you have learned in training will help you not only on the job but in your personal life as well. Many of these skills will have applicability in your future professional role, whatever it may be. The reward for helping to make a positive difference for others as you serve in the peer educator role is great! However, in the final analysis, you will be the primary beneficiary of your helping interactions. Helping others grow is, in itself, a personal growth-promoting activity.

References

Astin, A. *What Matters in College? Four Critical Years Revisited.* San Francisco: Jossey-Bass, 1993.

Berg, J. H., and Wright-Buckley, C. "Effects of Racial Similarity and Interviewer Intimacy in a Peer Counseling Analogue." *Journal of Counseling Psychology*, 1988, *35*, 377–384.

Borton, T. *Reach, Touch, and Teach.* New York: McGraw-Hill, 1970.

Brenden, M. A. "Pioneering New Support Systems for Non-Traditional Baccalaureate Students." *NACADA Journal*, 1986, *6*, 77–82.

Brislin, R. *Understanding Culture's Influence on Behavior.* Orlando: Harcourt Brace, 1993.

Brown, W. F. "Effectiveness of Paraprofessionals: The Evidence." *Personnel and Guidance Journal*, 1974, *53*(4), 257–263.

Burke, C. "Developing a Program for Student Peer Educators." *Journal of College Student Development*, 1989, *30*, 368–369.

Burns, J. M. *Leadership.* New York: HarperCollins, 1978.

Carkhuff, R. R. "Differential Functioning of Lay and Professional Helpers." *Journal of Counseling Psychology*, 1968, *15*, 117–126.

Carkhuff, R. R. *Helping and Human Relations.* Austin, Tex.: Holt, Rinehart and Winston, 1969.

Carkhuff, R. R., and Truax, C. B. "Lay Mental Health Counseling: The Effects of Lay Group Counseling." *Journal of counseling Psychology*, 1965, *29*, 426–431.

Carns, A. W., Carns, M. R., and Wright, J. "Students as Paraprofessionals in Four-Year Colleges and Universities: Current Practice Compared to Prior Practice." *Journal of College Student Development*, 1993, *34*, 358–363.

Cartwright, D., and Zander, A. "Issues and Basic Assumptions." In D. Cartwright and A. Zander (eds.), *Group Dynamics.* New York: HarperCollins, 1968.

Chickering, A. W., and Reisser, L. *Education and Identity.* (2nd ed.) San Francisco: Jossey-Bass, 1993.

De Bono, E. *New Think.* New York: Avon Books, 1971. (Originally published 1967.)

De Bono, E. *PO: A Device for Successful Thinking.* New York: Simon & Schuster, 1972.

Egan, G. *The Skilled Helper: A Model for Systematic Helping and Interpersonal Relating.* Belmont, Calif.: Wadsworth, 1975.

Ender, S. C. "Students as Paraprofessionals." In T. K. Miller, R. B. Winstead Jr., and W. R. Mendenhall (eds.), *Administration and Leadership in Student Affairs: Actualizing Student Development In Higher Education.* Muncie, Ind.: Accelerated Development, 1983.

Ender, S. C., Saunders-McCaffrey, S., and Miller, T. K. *Students Helping Students: A Training Manual for Peer Helpers on the College Campus.* Athens, Ga.: Student Development Associates, 1979.

Ender, S. C., and Winston, R. B., Jr. (eds.) *Students as Paraprofessional Staff.* San Francisco: Jossey-Bass, 1984.

Erikson, E. H. *Childhood and Society.* (2nd ed.) New York: Norton, 1963.

Evans, N. J. "Theories of Student Development." In S. K. Komives, D. B. Woodard Jr., and Associates, *Student Services: A Handbook for the Profession.* (3rd ed.) San Francisco: Jossey-Bass, 1996.

Feldman, K. A., and Newcomb, T. M. *The Impact of College on Students: An Analysis of Four Decades of Research.* Vol. 1. San Francisco: Jossey-Bass, 1970.

Fiedler, R. *A Theory of Leadership Effectiveness.* New York: McGraw-Hill, 1967.

Frisz, R. H., and Lane, J. R. "Student User Evaluations of Peer Adviser Services." *Journal of College Student Personnel,* 1987, *28,* 241–245.

Fuhriman, A., and Burlingame, G. M. "Consistency of Matter: A Comparative Analysis of Individual and Group Process Variables." *Counseling Psychologists,* 1990, *18*(1), 6–63.

Gazda, G. M., Asbury, F., Balzer, F. J., Childers, W. C., and Walters, R. P. *Human Relations Development: A Manual for Educators.* (2nd ed.) Needham Heights, Mass.: Allyn & Bacon, 1977.

Gilligan, C. A. *In a Different Voice.* Cambridge, Mass.: Harvard University Press, 1982.

Hanf, M. B. "Mapping: A Technique for Translating Reading into Thinking." *Journal of Reading,* 1971, *14,* 225–230, 270.

Hershey, P., and Blanchard, K. *Management of Organizational Behavior: Utilizing Human Resources.* Upper Saddle River, N.J.: Prentice Hall, 1977.

Herzberg, F. "One More Time: How Do You Motivate Employees?" *Harvard Business Review*, 1968, 46(1), 53–62.

Hesselbein, F., Goldsmith, M., and Beckhard, R. *The Leader of the Future: New Visions, Strategies, and Practices for the Next Era*. San Francisco: Jossey-Bass, 1996.

Hofstede, G. *Cultures and Organizations, Software of the Mind*. New York: McGraw-Hill, 1991.

House, J., and Mitchell, T. R. "Path-Goal Theory of Leadership." *Journal of Contemporary Business*, 1974, 3(4), 81–98.

Kouzes, J. W., and Posner, B. Z. *The Leadership Challenge: How to Get Extraordinary Things Done in Organizations*. San Francisco: Jossey-Bass, 1987.

Kramer, G. L., and Hardy, H. N. "Facilitating the Freshman Experience." *College and University*, 1985, 60, 242–251.

Lenihan, G., and Kirk, W. G. "Using Student Paraprofessionals in the Treatment of Eating Disorders." *Journal of Counseling & Development*, 1990, 68, 332–335.

Lewin, K. *Field Theory in Social Sciences*. New York: HarperCollins, 1951.

Lonabocker, L. "Freshman Registration and Advisement." *College and University*, 1987, 62, 341–344.

Materniak, G. "Student Paraprofessionals in the Learning Skills Center." In S. C. Ender and R. B. Winston Jr. (eds.), *Students as Paraprofessional Staff*. San Francisco: Jossey-Bass, 1984.

Miller, T. K., and Prince, J. S. *The Future of Student Affairs: A Guide to Student Development for Tomorrow's Higher Education*. San Francisco: Jossey-Bass, 1977.

Newton, F. B. "Community Building Strategies with Student Groups." In F. Newton and K. L. Ender (eds.), *Student Development Practices: Strategies for Making a Difference*. Springfield, Ill.: Thomas, 1980.

Newton, F. B. "The Stressed Student: How Can We Help?" *About Campus*, 1998, 3(2), 4–10.

Newton, F. B., and Rieman, A. J. "Improving the Functioning of College Groups, or Doctor Can You Keep the Patient Healthy?" *Southern College Personnel Association Journal*, 1978, 1(1), 27–36.

Newton, F. B., and Wilson, M. W. "The Presence and Function of Metaphor in Supervision Sessions: An Intensive Case Study Using Process Methodology." *Journal of College Student Development*, 1991, 32(5), 455–465.

Paige, M. "On the Nature of Intercultural Experiences and Intercultural Education." In Paige, M. (ed.), *Education for the Intercultural Experience*. Yarmouth, Me.: Intercultural Press, 1993.

Pascarella, E. T., and Terenzini, P. T. *How College Affects Students: Findings and Insights from Twenty Years of Research*. San Francisco: Jossey-Bass, 1991.

Pauk, W. (1997). *How to Study in College*. (6th ed.) Boston: Houghton Mifflin.

Posthuma, B. W. *Small Groups in Counseling and Therapy*. Needham Heights, Mass.: Allyn & Bacon, 1996.

Powell, J. R., Pyler, S. A., Dickerson, B. A., and McClellan, S. D. *The Personnel Assistant in College Resident Halls*. Boston: Houghton Mifflin, 1969.

Presser, N. R., Miller, T. B., and Rapin, L. S. "Peer Consultants: A New Role for Student Paraprofessionals." *Journal of College Student Personnel*, 1984, *25*, 321–326.

Prince, G. M. "The Operational Mechanisms of Synectics." In G. A. Davis and J. A. Scott (eds.), *Training Creative Thinking*. Austin, Tex.: Holt, Rinehart and Winston, 1971.

Russell, J. H., and Skinkle, R. R. "Evaluation of Peer Adviser Effectiveness." *Journal of College Student Development*, 1990, *31*, 388–394.

Russell, J. H., and Thompson, D. "Evaluation of a Program of Peer Helping for First-Year Students." *Journal of College Student Personnel*, 1987, *28*, 330–336.

Shepherd, J. F. *RSVP: The College Reading, Study, and Vocabulary Program*. (4th ed.) Boston: Houghton Mifflin, 1992.

Shertzer, B., and Stone, B. *Fundamentals of Counseling*. (2nd ed.) Boston: Houghton Mifflin, 1974.

Stevens-Long, J. *Adult Life, Developmental Processes*. Palo Alto, Calif.: Mayfield, 1984.

Triandis, H. *The Analysis of Subjective Culture*. New York: Wiley, 1972.

Vigoda, R. "On Today's Campus, Stress is a Major Subject." *Philadelphia Inquirer*, Dec. 13, 1998, pp. 1, 23.

Von Oech, R. *A Kick in the Seat of the Pants*. New York: HarperCollins, 1986.

Waldo, M. "Primary Prevention in University Residence Halls: Paraprofessional-Led Relationship Enhancement Groups for College Roommates." *Journal of Counseling and Development*, 1989, *67*, 465–472.

White, R., and Lippitt, R. "Leader Behavior and Member Reactions in Three Social Climates." In D. Cartwright and A. Zander (eds.), *Group Dynamics: Research and Theory*. New York: HarperCollins, 1968.

Winston, R. B., Jr., and Ender, S. C. "Use of Student Paraprofessionals in Divisions of College Student Affairs." *Journal of Counseling and Development*, 1988, *66*, 466–473.

Yalom, I. D. *The Theory and Practice of Group Psychotherapy*. New York: Basic Books, 1995.

Yamauchi, G. "Students Helping Students: The Emergence of Paraprofessionals in Campus Activities." *Campus Activities Programming,* 1986, *25,* 430–436.

Zunker, V. G., and Brown, W. F. "Comparative Effectiveness of Student and Professional Counselors." *Personnel and Guidance Journal,* 1966, *44*(7), 738–743.

Index